HOPE

for Every

HOME

Your Brave Each Day!

John & Lee
Guadagno

Printed by
Companion Press
P.O. Box 310
Shippensburg, PA 17257-0310

ISBN 1-56043-227-6

For Worldwide Distribution
Printed in the U.S.A.

THIS BOOK IS DEDICATED...

To the reader, in the hope that you will experience the love, power and faithfulness of God that my family and I have experienced for many years;

To my children – Joe, Jason, Jimmy and Jennifer, to whom words of gratitude are not enough for helping to make many difficult years, due to the on-duty injury, more bearable. You embraced the challenges and together in God's love, we have overcome insurmountable odds. Also to my daughter-in-love Michelle and my grandchildren Meaghan, Olivia, Joey and Johnny for the wonderful part each of you plays in my life;

To my wife, who has always shown me how God loves through a human being, and has been my closest friend, encourager, nurse and best supporter. Thank you for choosing to see me through the eyes of a loving God;

And to the Lord Jesus Christ, the cornerstone of my life, Who is forever changing me and inspiring me to reach out to others through many avenues, including this book.

ACKNOWLEDGEMENTS

I would like to extend my sincere gratitude to Rev. Thomas F. Reid of the Tabernacle in Orchard Park, New York, whose Godly character and ministry have been inspiring to me even from a distance, when I was unable to physically attend his loving church environment.

Special mention must also be made of the men and women who pioneered Christian television and radio, and the many who minister in Word and song who have played a part in my healing process, especially those who persevered to bring Christian television to Western New York.

Many thanks also to Chaplain Bill Flick, who was the first to share the good news with me 1978, to Chaplain Roger Rainville, and Jim Anthony for always being there.

To Bill and the late Jackie Karle who loved and influenced me like parents and from whom I gleaned so much over the years.

Thanks also to our mothers, Olivia Pavicich and the late Margaret Guadagno, for their constant encouragement, and to Olivia for proofreading this text.

Additionally, special thanks to a woman who reflects the grace, wisdom and mercy of God, my long-time friend Barbara Minniefield, pastor of Sword of the Spirit Ministries in Buffalo, New York. She has always spoken into my life, encouraging my faith and my calling.

God bless all of you for your influence and for encouraging the writing of this book.

ENDORSEMENTS

"This book addresses the deep needs of individuals in all family situations, offering practical advice and information on how to use God's building blocks for successful families. It will help repair the fractured family relationships of our age, offering hope not only to this generation but to future generations as well. Courageous work…"

-Garth W. Coonce, President and Founder
Tri-State Christian Television Network

"I highly endorse this book to all my colleagues, especially those representing the Body of Christ in urban areas. It's a text book to bring in the urban harvest. Guadagno's work assists us with day-to-day ethical decision making, while helping each of us determine our Christian worth. Excellent for study groups."

-Bishop William A. Dockery
Memorial Temple Christian Ministries
Church of God In Christ

"The healing of the devastation that took place in the author's life and family is a glaring example of the power of God to change lives, restore relationships…extremely vulnerable, open and honest. It's real! It's practical! It's hopeful!"   -Rev. Barbara Minniefield
Pastor, Sword of the Spirit Ministries
Christian International

"We found ourselves saying 'This is what we would say' in counseling situations...practical down to earth advice...valuable asset to any family, blended or not."

-Rev. Jeff Hokenson
Pastor, Pioneer Christian Fellowship
Elim Fellowship

"It is my great privilege to recommend this book to you. If you are in a hurting or hurtful place in your life, this book will help you come into a place of understanding and healing. If you are facing the challenges that a blended family brings, this is a resource that you must have. God has brought a message to the Body of Christ through John Guadagno that you will want to share with others."

-John W. Bowers
Pastor, Grace Fellowship Church, Erie, PA
Tri-State Apostolic Region
Coordinator for Christian International

CONTENTS

FOREWORD

John and Lee Guadagno have given the world a tremendous gift in their new book. This outstanding manuscript details the problems and the solutions they found as they have become "partners with God" in developing a successful blended family. This work is a "must" for not only couples who are wrestling with the problems of the blended family, but those who are discovering the complexity of marriage in our contemporary culture. Biblical solutions work in every situation!

I have had the privilege of knowing this amazing Christian family for over twenty years. I have seen them go through problems that would have challenged the faith of the most devoted among us. I have watched as they not only survived these problems, but they succeeded in applying the truth of the scripture, and the wonder of their relationship with God in every situation. They truly demonstrate what it means to be "MORE THAN CONQUERORS".

This book is destined to impact the contemporary family and the challenges of marriage within the context of contemporary culture. Once you begin reading it, you will not be able to put it down. It is a true story. I can attest to that fact. It truly identifies the Biblical solutions to family relationships in a way no contemporary writer has ever done, because it is their own true life story, and THEY KNOW THE GOSPEL WORKS!

Dr. Thomas F. (Tommy) Reid
Senior Pastor, Full Gospel Tabernacle, Orchard Park, New York   Assemblies of God

PREFACE

It is God's will for you and your family to be made whole, to live with hope, healing and a sense of purpose and destiny (Jeremiah. 29:11). You can overcome obstacles and fulfill God's plan by determining to do so and being obedient to the principles He has outlined for living. You can't go back and relive your life, but you can choose the path you will follow from this moment on. You do not have to live in defeat, condemnation, rejection or shame due to your past. In God's eyes, forgiven is forgotten (Psalm 103:12). Each chapter in this book deals with a specific aspect of the will of God for you. Implementing these truths will produce healing, direction and power to pursue God's will in your life. As you go down this road, there will be curves, hills, major potholes, detours and even some signs that say "bridge closed". Don't stay upset or frustrated with these, but begin to recognize that God's wisdom is far superior to your own. A "bridge closed" sign means that He has a different way for you to go right now. Take some pressure off yourself by accepting that fact, and allow yourself a season of healing if you have not done so already.

We all know someone who has had a broken bone. In the process of healing, you go to the doctor who sets a cast and gives specific directions on the do's and don'ts of the healing process. The cast is uncomfortable, and it's awkward. You are self-conscious. The limb itches and you want to cut the cast off. However, if you follow your own will instead of the physician's, you will only add hurt and more time to the healing process. You must have a change of lifestyle in order to accomplish every day tasks with the cast on. The same is true with emotional healing. The Great Physician knows best. One of the changes that must be made is to be thankful that you are under His care. Be thankful that, even though the process is uncomfortable, you know that the "limb" will finally be stronger than it was before. This process takes patience. God's will takes patience. It is better for us to live with the uncomfortable feeling for a season and become healed than to live an entire lifetime of failure and defeat.

There is purpose, destiny and healing for the divorced and remarried. A blended family is not a second-class family. You do not have to be ashamed or guilt-ridden due to your past. Following the Word of God and the will of God, you can find your purpose and then impact the world around you. We live in a society in which multitudes are hurting due to the trauma of divorce. We have the ability to bring hope, healing and restoration to these families through our own healing. Do not allow your past to dictate your future!

Before discussing aspects of the blended family, I must give you a brief personal history so you may better understand and appreciate the awesome love and mercy that is available to you if you are willing to yield and change.

Police work was my chosen career. Even in my high school yearbook, fellow students wrote messages about my becoming a police officer with a successful career. My work soon became an idol to me as I ate, slept and lived police work. I had a six month old daughter when my marriage of about seven years broke up. I was full of hatred, bitterness, jealousy and anger. I did not trust anyone after that, especially women. To the natural eye, I had a good job, good health, financial stability and could date anyone I wanted, which looked very appealing to the men at work. They thought I had everything that made for happiness, but in reality, I was miserable, lonely and angry. However, I realized later that even then, I was being prepared for the years ahead. Yes, even when there is tremendous pain, suffering and trial, God is there with you. Now if you have submitted your life to Him, He has access to heal your past and lead you into a great future (Luke 4:18).

One midnight shift in July of 1978, I was assigned a partner, which was unusual, as I worked alone most of the time. My partner was driving and, several hours into our shift, we were involved in a head-on collision with a drunk driver and were both sent to the hospital. I was seen and released but the doctor put me off work for a period of time to recover from my injuries. Several days later, I woke up and got into my car with a strong urge to go to a particular part of our town, which led me to the home of an old high school friend whom I hadn't seen in many years. I did not know who lived in this house but as I pulled up, I found it was my old friend Bill who had just moved there three months before. I believe this urge to go there came from the Spirit of God. That day, my friend Bill shared with me the love of God through Jesus Christ. This was the first time in my life I had heard the simple message of the gospel. I committed my life to the lordship of Jesus Christ that day in Bill's living room. He invited me to a local church where my first pastor taught me to read and study the Bible for myself, to search the Word and put its concepts into practice. I went to work with the Bible on cassette tape and listened to those tapes in the police car between calls. The love of God began replacing the hatred that was in my heart and I began undergoing real transformation.

It was at this church that I met the lovely woman I would marry several years later. She had three young sons that she had been raising alone for some time. My lifestyle was beginning to change as I allowed God to cultivate my mind and heart. As I learned to praise Him and thank Him, my words, my actions, my personality and my countenance were changing. Others began to take notice of the real difference in my life, and the men at work saw that my bitterness was being replaced with kindness and patience.

On October 31, 1981 another event occurred that changed my life. I went to work that day with the ability to bench press three hundred pounds, in good physical, mental and spiritual health, knowing God's presence and practicing His ways. I was assigned to a train derailment and worked a sixteen hour shift. We evacuated about five thousand people from their homes due to a large fire and chemical fumes that filled the air. During the second eight hour shift, I was detailed to the scene of the derailment while all other officers were released. I did not know that the tank car next to me was filled with toxic chemicals. As a work crew attempted to lift the car onto the track, it fell emitting a cloud of toxic gas, forcing everyone to run from the car. As I was running, I felt fatigued and short of breath, but didn't think much of it, as it was already about the twelfth hour of my double shift. As the scene was secured, I continued working till my shift was over. I didn't sleep well that night but didn't think that was unusual given the events of the day. However, I was very weak, short of breath and I passed out the next day, so I reported off work thinking I had the flu. I made an appointment with my doctor and he immediately detected an irregularity in my heartbeat. He gave me a note to be off work and I was soon hospitalized. I was not aware at that time of the extent of my injury and believed I would be back to work in a short time.

I have since seen twenty doctors, had extensive medical testing and found that the toxic chemical damaged my central nervous system (brain and spinal cord) affecting many of my internal organs and body systems. I later found out that the irregular heart beat was due to damage to the nerves which supply the heart. I began to suffer from insomnia, nightmares and the inability to rest or relax. I experienced a loss of muscle mass with extreme weakness and fatigue, loss of coordination on my left side and severe diminishing of motor skills. For example, I couldn't put two objects together like a nut and bolt, or coordinate movements using both hands. I began to have difficulty reading and concentrating, and suffered bouts of severe depression. Memory loss and problems with speech and language skills were very frustrating, and temperature changes and high humidity made breathing difficult. I was diagnosed with Post-Traumatic Stress Disorder, with recurring nightmares, mood swings and emotional flare-ups. I have documentation from a treating physician stating that it was my spiritual strength that helped me recover psychologically from the chemical injury. Not being able to do the work I loved was one thing, but not being able to shovel snow, change a tire or carry my little girl was something else.

Lee and I married five weeks after the accident, still unaware of the extent of my injury. In addition, we faced the challenges that face all blended families. However, no circumstance that comes into your life is any match for God's mercy and the power of His Word. Even though my livelihood, my health and my sense of self-worth were stripped from me, the presence of God and the power of His Word could never be taken away. I believe that this book will bring you tremendous hope. We and our adult children live today in the liberty of obstacles overcome by faith, patience and obedience.

Enjoying the kind of relationships God intended is well worth the trials you may now be facing. Remember that no weapon formed against you will prosper and the Spirit of God will never leave you, so begin where you are by choosing to be thankful and joyful (Isaiah 54:17; Hebrews 13:5). There are great days ahead for you and your family if you are willing to forgive, put the past behind you and put Biblical principles into action in your every day life.

In my years as a policeman, I investigated a variety of tragedies – child abuse, abuse of women by males who simply refuse to become men, highway disasters and violence in every form imaginable. I was called upon many times to go into the homes of veterans who were exposed to toxic chemicals in the Viet Nam War. These men would go through much of what I experienced these last years from chemical exposure. It was very painful for me to subdue these heroes of ours so that they could be taken to hospitals for medical help. What was the cause of their heartache and hurt? It was the same as mine. We simply obeyed our superior officers, trying to bring peace and safety to a turbulent situation.

Raising a blended family with all the difficulties and frustrations of my injury, I could have chosen the victim mentality as an excuse for not changing, but I could not do so for very long. Instead I have found hope, healing, purpose and renewed vision in God, and so can you. Yes, we have questions. We cry. Maybe out of God's love and kindness He reveals some of the answers to us. Whether or not He does, He's given us enough answers through His written Word and His Spirit to bring us out of these tragic situations into a productive life under His guidance. As you will read, Christ-like character began to be developed in me, not when I was at the peak of my health, my career or my family life, but at the lowest point of all. So I encourage you to start where you are, even if you can only wake up in the morning and draw breath. Start by being thankful for that.

As I talk about issues in this book, I will refer often to prayer. I mean simply communicating with God and being open to His direction for your life. As you read His Word, empty yourself out of hurts, questions and confusion. Be aware that God will direct you through the Bible, through circumstances and through other people as He orchestrates all things for your good (Romans 8:28). Take time at the beginning of each day to talk to Him and as you work through the day, be aware of His being with you and His desire to guide you (Proverbs 3:5, 6). Sometime when it is quiet, perhaps in the evening, write down your thoughts and prayers and date them, and you will see in time, as you look back, how God has answered your prayers. Sometimes He will speak in the stillness of your heart, simply impressing you to do something or to take a certain direction. He may impress you to do something good for someone who has hurt you, strengthening the forgiveness between you. Do not become guilt-ridden about the amount of time you spend in prayer, but rather learn to express yourself to God and "listen" for His answers all the time. As you spend more time in the Word and become more aware of His presence, you will enjoy this fellowship more and your relationship will grow.

Yes, books, tapes and seminars on prayer are helpful; however, a season of crisis is when most people develop an effective prayer life. It's when we place God and His priorities first in our lives and keep them there continually that prayer will become the wisdom and power of God moving through us (Jeremiah 29:13). There will be times, as your prayer life develops, when God will make you aware of events in your children's lives before they occur. He will enable you to talk to them about issues they are struggling with and head off some problems before they amount to much. A well-developed prayer life will have long-reaching effects on successful parenting.

You will find that the Lord wants to bless you, meaning simply to pour His favor on you and to give you a sense of well-being through covenant relationship. This is the special relationship we have with God made possible by the sacrifice of Jesus (Hebrews 8:6-13; Jeremiah 31:31-34). As we become secure in God's love, we will discover that He has given us talents, gifts, favor with people and many other blessings. We will also discover that we have the ability to bless those around us with a smile, a thankful spirit, a word, our resources and many other things. God wants to prosper your life and bring you goodness (Psalm 1:1-3; III John v. 2). He wants to fill you with love, power and a sound mind (II Timothy 1:7). All you need to do is choose to have a Christ-like attitude and yield to the work of the Holy Spirit. Learn to be thankful and choose to rejoice and you will overcome any obstacle in your path (Romans 8:37).

When our daughter was about three years old, I began to play the "Thank you" game with her. I would take her hand, go for a walk and we would take turns thanking the Lord for His love and kindness in simple ways. She would say "Thank you Jesus for the sunshine", for example, or for flowers or for her teddy bear. I would thank Him for hugs, for brothers or for my special little girl. This began a life teaching for her on being thankful in every season of life. She is now twenty-two years old and fondly remembers thanking the Lord for love, for a new doll and a bicycle. More importantly, she learned to thank the Lord for every breath of fresh air, for health and other things money can not buy. This takes time to develop. Take a pad and pencil and start a "thank you" list. If you add something to it faithfully every day, your "thank you" list will soon outweigh your "need" list. You will understand the goodness of God in a new way, even if you are at your lowest point.

A foundation of prayer and thankfulness gives God the framework on which to build a work of grace in your life. Your destiny is to be in relationship with God as He ordained long before you were born (Ephesians 1:4,5). You have a purpose to fulfill in life and He wants you to know His will or desired direction to help you accomplish it. He has placed gifts and abilities within you according to that purpose, and He simply wants you to trust Him (Ephesians 4:7,8). The fact that you have had a broken marriage does not mean that God's plan for you has been terminated. Let me share some stories from my life and some principles from God's Word that demonstrate these truths.

CHAPTER ONE

COMMITMENT-COUNTING THE COST

It is the will of God for us to be committed to the care, well-being and growth of our families (I Timothy 5:8). You must also be committed to particular adjustments in the blended family that first-time married couples do not have to make. An example is that the remarried couple usually does not have the luxury of getting to know each other as husband and wife without the presence and responsibility of children. There is an instant family with many new dynamics. This should have been an important consideration before the wedding. Whether or not it was, there are some things you can do to help integrate all family members and strengthen your marriage.

The concept of counting the cost or commitment level for marriage has been slowly eroding in our nation for the last several decades. There has been widespread breakdown of traditional family values through many different avenues. We are encouraged to be self-centered individuals seeking instant gratification and always putting our own welfare first. However, you and I must resolve to resist these influences in determining the longevity, the productivity and the character of our families (Romans 12:2). We must take the Biblical standard for our own in order to realize the blessing of God in our homes.

The blended family demands a high level of commitment in every area. One of the challenges is parenting children who are not biologically yours. Another is maintaining a working relationship with the child/children's other parent. All members of the family will need time to work out their feelings from the break-up of old relationships and time to establish new ones. The future may look confusing, not only to the children, but to the new couple as well. Even if these things seem bigger than life right now, there is hope, and you don't have to go through life without any real goals for success. We must choose the higher road of faith and commitment to the Lord and His attitude of living in order to see real change. When I use the word faith, I mean trust in the Lord and in His written Word, not faith in something vague or a hope that maybe something will change. Faith is trust in God that once you commit yourself to Him and to His ways, things WILL change. The responsibility might seem overwhelming right now, but resting – in God's faithfulness, in His Word and His promises, in the fact that He loves you and your family – is a major step toward giving Him access to the "nuts and bolts" of your life and letting His power loose in your circumstances (Proverbs 3:1-4). You will be able to come together as husband and wife and create an atmosphere of peace, joy and cooperation in the home that will allow all members of the family to grow, to heal and even to fail at times. No one will know success or contentment until failure has been met head on. We will make mistakes and so will our children, so be ready to give and ask for lots of forgiveness!

I have used myself as an example in this book time and time again, of missing the mark and coming short of what it means to be a man yielded to the Lord. However, that is past and since I determined in my heart to allow God to change me, I am no longer full of bitterness, resentment or mistrust. The Lord has used many means to change my attitude and direction, and He will do the same for you and the generations after you. Your decisions will have far-reaching effects (Deuteronomy 30:9).

It takes a great emotional commitment to make a blended family work, especially for those who have a failed marriage in their past. You may feel as though you are destined to fail again, but this is not so. The truth is that God wants your marriage to succeed more than you do at times. We must be willing to trust again. This involves a healing process and learning to let go. It's difficult to trust someone with your feelings after having been betrayed or abandoned. Sometimes even after the death of a spouse, there may be residual, even unconscious, anger at being "left" by the one we loved. All these feelings make it difficult to commit emotionally again. We keep ourselves somewhat in reserve so we can't be hurt again. It takes time to develop trust. This is one critical reason why we must have a healing season after a broken relationship. It is impossible to cement new ties over cracks and breaks in our emotions.

You must ask yourself if you are willing to make the necessary sacrifices to parent someone else's children as if they were your own. Many times, children of divorce will have a bias against you because, in their eyes, you are taking the place of their birth parent. Are you emotionally stable enough to anticipate this, and to help them work through the upheaval in their lives? It costs something. Have you counted the cost financially? Have you considered the spiritual cost of leading a blended family? Can you model for them the desired character you wish to instill in them? This includes the right way to correct mistakes. We're not perfect, but we can live lives that demonstrate the love and compassion of God in us. What will this cost you in time and involvement with a local church to help meet your family's needs? What about extended family obligations, employment, social and personal needs? There is much to consider.

Look at the opportunities for your new family to love, to grow and to create a sense of who you are together. You may experience feelings of wanting to quit at times. Don't. It's worth it to stay the course and I will talk more about that in the following chapters. Following through on your commitments to your family will take you off the path of disappointment and destruction and bring you into unity, strength and a future full of great purpose and satisfaction.

With the Lord's guidance, whatever you dream can become reality for you through work, dedication, sacrifice and the many miracles and blessings you will experience on your road of faith (Psalm 37:4,5).

Yes, you have come from diverse backgrounds, hurts and disappointments. However, you and your family have the opportunity for wholeness ahead. Anticipate your own attitudes changing into more Christ-centered ones as you humble yourself. There are no problems, events or circumstances in life that can cause real devastation to you except the unwillingness to embrace God's attitude and make it your own. That unwillingness will always spell defeat. You can have a sound family that is solidly together if you build on the right foundation (Proverbs 24:3,4).

Single and Contemplating Marriage

If you are a single individual contemplating marriage today, I encourage you to follow the few basic principles and guidelines in the following chapters. Before we married, my wife Lee was a single mother for almost nine years and I was a single father for almost four years. We would both encourage you to allow the Word of God to guide your direction in this all-important issue of choosing a mate. Ladies, let the Lord be your husband; and men, He will meet all your needs too. It's critical to FIND YOUR IDENTITY AND CONTENTMENT IN GOD before you try to establish an intimate relationship with someone else. Take time before you marry to allow Him to bring healing, strength and stability into your life. One of the ways to accomplish this is by determining to be content (I Timothy 6:6). Most single people want to be married and most married people want to be single! What is missing is the spirit of contentment.

4

Being a single parent can be very frustrating and it's an awesome responsibility. You sacrifice and provide the best you can for your children and, often times, the other parent is not around or is not living up to his or her obligations to the children. Allow the Lord to be your provision, your protector and your guide. A strong local church should be an asset to you, not only through its teaching ministry but also in Godly men and women who can be active participants in your child's upbringing. Don't buy into the lie that you have to get married out of loneliness or in order to give your children a father figure or mother figure. Your children are better off having you – sound, stable and mature in the Lord – raising them with church support, than having you marry someone who is not prepared to be a Godly influence in their lives.

Ladies, do not compromise your stand in the Lord for any male. It's sad to say but we often read or hear about children who are abused, neglected or worse when their mothers put their need for companionship ahead of their own children's protection and well-being. Please do not compromise your moral stand for anyone. If an individual is truly a Godly man, he will not only wait for you till marriage, but he will show you that he is ready, willing and able to provide for you, to care for your children and to share the responsibilities of child rearing in the ways of the Lord. If you are dating someone who does not want this – and he could be a Christian – simply get out of the relationship, wait on God and go on with your life. You and your children do not need any more emotional wreckage. They can and will be made whole by your example and influence, with the help of a loving church environment. If the Lord does bring a Godly man into your life, that's a plus, but in the mean time, do not compromise. Men, this is also true for you. If you are looking for a wife and perhaps a mother for your children, you need a strong Godly woman to meet the challenge.

5

You may struggle with negative feelings because you are unsuccessful at being two parents to your children. I felt the same way, but I finally rested with being the one parent I was capable of being. By doing so, we take the pressure off of our children and ourselves. The Lord will provide the other aspect of fathering or mothering for your children in His own way and time (Psalm 68:5). The same principles apply to an individual who has never been married and is contemplating marriage. You might meet a wonderful, Godly man or woman who has children from a previous marriage, and you are not sure you can handle the responsibility. Again, I caution you to work through a season of healing with this person and with the children to be sure that you are each prepared to deal with the unique challenges ahead. Remember, what you see on the surface is only the tip of the iceberg. When you are married and living under the same roof, the pressures of everyday life will bring many things to the surface. I hope you recognize by now that if God can change me after what I have been through and make ours a loving and productive family, He can do it for you too. God is no respecter of persons, but you must be willing to count the cost (Acts 10:34). If you know in your heart that you can not raise someone else's children, please get out of the relationship you are in before you do harm to someone else and his or her children. You are better off to walk away on a good note than to get married and provide an atmosphere of tension, anger and possibly another divorce. This marriage will not work if you are not able to embrace the children and their needs. Allow the Lord to bring healing to your life and be content with the state in which you find yourself. Go through this process with counsel from your pastor or other person who has been in the same situation, and keep your eyes focused on the goodness of God. He knows your need and wants you to be whole. Give yourself time. You can be whole as a single person, too!

Contentment is also accomplished by learning not to compare yourself with others around you in the sense that they are dating or married and you are not. Be very cautious. Just because a single individual attends church does not mean that this person is an appropriate marriage partner for you. Please keep this in your mind and heart, and don't allow your emotions to run away with you. Do not compare yourself with, or be envious of others but allow the Lord to work in your life and love you to wholeness before you get involved in a romantic relationship. Let's say that you are a student of the Word. You are an obedient Christian who practices tithing and walking in forgiveness, for example. However, these values are not important to your prospective spouse who is also a believer. This is probably not the person you should marry right now because these things are indications of the heart attitude. There are many believers who are unhappy because they are not evenly bound together with their spouses. Being evenly bound together does not simply mean going to church together. It means that both of you are committed to the things of God, the ways of God, and the will of God – to change and growth. Perhaps this individual will mature in time to embrace these Biblical attitudes, but you can not assume this, nor can you marry with the idea that you will change him or her. By keeping your eyes on the goodness of God and the direction He is taking you, you will allow Him to change you and to bring an individual into your life with whom you can be evenly paired. God's desire is to prepare you to truly love someone – someone with whom you can laugh, cry and share all of life's experiences. At the same time, He will prepare someone who loves Him for lifelong commitment to you. It is as much about being the right partner as it is about marrying the right partner. Walk slowly and cautiously, letting God prepare you for marriage with someone of high, Biblical standards. This is one situation where an ounce of prevention can spare you many years of misery. It's worth the wait!

Married and Contemplating Separation

As you are aware, we live in a society that is not family friendly any more. At one time, our nation was family oriented as we were founded on Judeo-Christian values. We could once send our children to school and believe that our parental authority and religious traditions were not being undermined. There are now many strong influences around us promoting violence, adultery and self-centeredness of every form, bombarding our thoughts and decision-making processes as we go through life's trials. Even the banking institutions have changed their philosophy. Until ten or fifteen years ago, bank officers would sit with you and be sure you could pay your obligation before granting you credit. That's not how it works today. We are all deluged with mailings and phone calls for pre-approved credit. You don't even have to have a job to get a credit card. Even my mother, who has been with the Lord for over six years now, gets mail and phone calls from credit card companies! Not only did we make proper notifications at the time of her death, but we have even moved to a new location! I think this demonstrates a philosophy of putting people under bondage to easy credit and high interest.

I mention this because the two main reasons married couples separate are financial pressure and unfaithfulness. As you work through this book, you will find insights on some of these problem areas. Even if you have to seek some help in resolving them, know that we serve a big God Who is able to restore any relationship when we are willing to humble ourselves and be changed.

It is sad to say but there are cases, even in Christian circles, where women and children live in fear and torment, subjected to severe abuse of all kinds, and there are many spouses who simply refuse to change. In such cases, these individuals need to take whatever steps are necessary to protect themselves and their children. Separation should be weighed out carefully. Be sure to seek Christian counsel. If you must go to the degree of legal separation to secure your safety and your children's, do so because God has called us to peace (John 14:27; I Corinthians 7:15b). A Christian counselor will advise you from the Word of God and the ways of God in the areas of forgiveness and communication, for example. If there is a separation for a short season, be sure there are specific reasons for it and specific goals to accomplish. We know some couples who have mutually agreed to separate for a specified time to reflect on their relationship, their problems, and their needs and were able to recognize again their love for and commitment to one another. With some outside help, a separation proved extremely beneficial in these cases. In any case, remember that God wants you whole, He wants you safe and He wants you to live without being in fear. I pray that the following chapters give you hope and some insights into changing your situation and gaining victory over your crisis. God loves you and will always show you the way when your desire is to follow Him.

Widowed and Remarried

You may be widowed and remarried and yet not have given yourself time to heal emotionally from your loss. Some women who are widowed remarry too soon because of financial pressure, especially when there are children at home. This is not to say that they do not love the person they married, but simply that the loss of a spouse can be overwhelming, not only with grief and fear but with new responsibilities. However, God's ability to heal and to give wisdom is not hampered in any way. Simply start where you are right now, and don't deny the season of life that you are in.

All of us have loved ones who will die before us. It is a greater tragedy if we allow the grief to render our minds and lives paralyzed, making us unable to go on. This occurs when we allow ourselves to lose all hope and purpose in life. Keep in mind that every human being that was ever born was created with a mission in life, the basis of which is to gain the compassion, the wisdom, the insight and the love of God. Simply, you and I can not allow a tragedy to prevent us from the will of God for us. We should not deny our feelings but allow ourselves time to work through them and be able to go on living. We are to lay aside all our fears, all our differences, all our prejudices and all our doubts. Death is like a dark night, but due to the death of our Lord Jesus Christ and His resurrection, morning comes. We have the opportunity to choose to use each morning that is afforded us for His purposes. His death appeared to be a great tragedy, but through it, we can choose to have abundant life, not just in eternity with Him, but here and now. Thank God, morning does come!

People grieve and heal in different lengths of time. There are no two people exactly alike. Mourning is difficult and painful. You experience things for the first time when you lose your spouse. Working, shopping, preparing meals will all seem different. Even though you might have children, everything will be different. The times that you would have shared with your spouse will be very lonely. Again, don't deny the feelings you are experiencing. Don't keep a smile on your face when you are hurting. Stop thinking about what other people say and do. They are not in your shoes or your season of life. Take the pressure off yourself and allow the process to begin. Writing daily what you think and feel may be helpful. Also, talk to the Lord and to others around you. Empty yourself out. If you go through seasons of anger, that's all right. As we are learning, we need to make sure the anger is dealt with. We might even, at times, become angry with God. No, God does not cause death or destruction. He gets blamed for many things He doesn't do, but He is big enough to handle your anger and mine. Perhaps you had faith and believed for healing for your loved one. Simply say, "Father, I do not understand why my spouse died. Forgive me for my anger". Don't deny your anger but begin to channel that energy into a productive healing process. Don't stay focused on it either. Deal with it and allow yourself to heal. The same is true with your children. Often times, they will experience anger following a death or divorce in the family. The principles are the same. The amount of time needed to heal is lengthened if we keep denying our emotions. The pain is real. Start where you are and permit God to heal and refill the empty, hurting places in your life as only He can.

Reminisce with immediate family members and friends about the good times as well as the times that were not so good. This will help you through your grieving. Not only cry together, but also laugh together, for you gain strength from one another as you share the experience. Laughing, crying, sharing memories and retaining certain keepsakes around the house are all part of the process. As stated before, the length of time needed to grieve and heal varies from person to person. Is one year, two years, three years enough? Each of us will handle the grief in a different way and can be helped by supportive people.

After the death of a loved one, or even during a prolonged illness while we give care at home or in the hospital, we may go through times when we do not have strength for other activities. Sometimes even long periods of prayer or Bible reading are too taxing on our short energy reserves. We may read or hear a teaching and be encouraged, but prayer during these times is often an attitude of heart that we carry with us all the time. The priority during these times is caring for a loved one in the strength God gives. He knows and understands this, and will give you a special grace and mercy. Some time after the death of a loved one, you will recognize that God was carrying you like a child through the period of illness, the grieving and even your own healing. You will realize that, just as a baby leans on its mother's bosom to draw strength, comfort and peace, you draw from God's warmth and love. There will be a day when He will put your feet on solid ground again. He will still be holding you but in a different way, allowing you to go on as you are learning to trust Him without your spouse. Our identity is intricately tied up in the person to whom we are married. After losing a spouse, we find ourselves empty and may feel that we have no direction in life. Feeling the emptiness of our great loss, finding our way alone is very different. As we become more at peace with who we are alone in Christ, the time, energy and love we gave to our spouse will be channeled to others.

Redirected Love

I have not lost a spouse in death but when my mother, who lived with us, died after a season with cancer, I decided to find other elderly women who were without family to get to know, respect and care for. For example, when paying my bill at a restaurant, if I see an elderly woman, I pay her bill as well without her knowing who paid it. It is just a way of showing respect as I would for my own mother. Doing these kinds of things also helps our own healing process because we are allowing love to flow through us to another human being. We are in awe as to how closely God does hold us during these times of our lives. We walk humbly with Him and depend on His grace. Yes, we miss our loved ones and always will, but we need not despair of life. Grieving takes time and we should not try to shortcut the process. It's important to talk about our loved ones, to cry, to laugh and to integrate our feelings and memories so that we can continue to live after their death. Never to speak of them or cry is just as abnormal as being preoccupied with them every moment.

With God's help and a couple of people you can really talk to, you will be able to assimilate this into your experience in a healthy way. When you are ready, you won't have to look very far to find people who need to be loved. As you begin to reach out again, you will find yourself strengthened and the spirit of the one you loved will live on through you in your acts of love and kindness to others.

Remember:
1. Commitment and sacrifice will bring change.
2. Don't compromise your moral stand.
3. Don't compare yourself with others.
4. Be content where you are right now.
5. Give yourself time to heal.

CHAPTER TWO

IT'S WORTH IT!

It is God's will for us to stay on course. Sometimes it feels like we face trials, trials and more trials. At the same time, we are accustomed to being told that we are number one. Our minds have been trained to be selfish and materially motivated to have instant success, to have what we want and to have it now, to do whatever feels good as if there were no right and wrong. Consider the following mindset.

"If I don't have the cash, I can charge what I want, even if I can't afford it, because I'm number one. It doesn't matter if the seller ever gets the money for the item or if I actually pay three times what it's worth in interest. And yes, once I have the instant gratification for a short season, it's okay to throw it away and get something else. I don't have to count the cost. What about all the relationships I am involved in at home, at work, at school? It's my needs, my wants, my desires that really matter, isn't it? If this marriage doesn't work out, I'll get out. I'll find someone who will love and understand me, and care for me. The kids, well, they will just have to understand. It's part of life. Our culture, our society approves. Commitment isn't really worth it, is it? It's my happiness that counts. I am number one, aren't I?"

No! Your wants and desires are not number one. They are not all that count. This may come as a surprise to some, but that is not the way God intended life to be. It is God's will – His way, His Word, His time-proven principles – that count. It's His wisdom, insight and love that have counted from eternity past and will count until eternity future. They are all that will change us. If you've been remarried, you can't go back, but you can start where you are right now. God is loving, merciful, tenderhearted and forgiving. Ask

Him for a new beginning. Act by faith upon His promises to forgive and forget and to make all things new (II Corinthians 5:17). Study His principles and learn and experience more of His character. He wants to reveal Himself to you.

You can build loving relationships that can last a lifetime. You can be an example to your children and others by determining to stick with your marriage and remain committed through the process of change. Yes, change is painful and difficult, but oh, so rewarding! One day at a time, you will gain strength, insight and wisdom to make the difference in your life, your children's lives and even the lives of your grandchildren down the road. You can not allow your feelings to dictate to you in the decision-making process. There will be times when it takes more than you expected and you may want to throw in the towel. However, don't yield to the feelings and temptations (II Corinthians 5:7). Stay focused on God's blueprint, putting His principles to work, and acting out of His love. He will grant you the ability to strengthen your marriage because He wants it to grow and prosper. It's worth the effort.

Becoming a parent overnight will bring seasons of adjustment to you and to the children. Some of what you will experience may be in the form of rejection, resistance and anger from children who have been hurt. Remember, you are not the cause of their hurt, but they do not realize that yet. They do not understand their own pain, but can begin to with your help. You will have disagreements with them and they may not want to listen to you because "you are not my mom or dad". These trying times can become seasons of great growth and change if you are willing to be painfully open and honest. The adjustments will be smoother if you help each other gain a greater understanding of who you are in the Lord's eyes and who you can be together. Be honest about your need for God to work in you, and your children will be more likely to be open about their need for God. Persevere.

You will have to deal with former spouses and, in some instances, children with whom you do not live. You will go through emotional ups and downs. You might be afraid. You might feel that you're a failure. You might feel rejected. You might want to give up on your new marriage and family, new responsibilities, and new privileges. I know. I felt that way many times, but I resisted the pull to quit. I stayed the course and didn't act on those feelings. It was worth it. Don't give up now.

Just because you're divorced and remarried doesn't mean you intended for your first marriage to end. You probably didn't get married with the idea of divorce in the back of your mind, although some people make you feel like you must have. Perhaps you have not taken the time to heal or have not wanted to deal with your own emotional pain and rejection from the broken relationship. Abuse, loss of trust, bitterness and unforgiveness are a few of the unresolved issues you may have. You may not feel like going to someone for assistance. You're working, you're busy, and you're married. You think it will be better this time. However, if you fail to close yourself in with God to find out who you are in Him and deal with these all-important issues, they will rise to the surface in many ways and be the defeat of your new relationships. As we are faithful to God's Word, and incidentally, even when we're not, He is faithful to us (II Thessalonians 3:3). However, the more we open ourselves up for this inner work, the sooner we will heal and stop responding to life out of our woundedness. We will not always look for someone else to prop us up, but rather will find our identity, strength and overcoming ability in the Lord. God will never let us down. He wants to heal all our wounds and deposit destiny and greatness in us.

No matter what you've accomplished or failed in until now, you can go on successfully. Your renewed sense of purpose will stabilize your family and keep you focused. You're on the right course. God's Word is true and powerful. The reading and application of His principles will put you on solid ground. You can demonstrate to others that God is loving, merciful and wise and that He wants families to be whole. The Lord wants to use you in whatever arena you find yourself. He wants you to influence others through Christ-like character at home, at work, in society. What is your sphere of influence? Are you willing to be used?

No matter what field you work in, the more you commit to God's ways, the more you will sense not only contentment but Godly wisdom and favor to handle day-to-day responsibilities. I could give you many examples of how this occurred when I was a police officer, but this one brief illustration will suffice to demonstrate that God desires men and women who are committed to Him in every walk of life.

One particular four-to-twelve shift in the summertime, I was assigned to work radar in an unmarked cruiser on certain roads. If there were any trouble calls, I was also to back up the other cars that were assigned these calls. About six p.m. a call came over the radio that there was a man about to jump off a bridge onto the New York State Thruway, so I immediately went to the scene. Upon my arrival, I saw a large crowd gathered and four or five marked patrol cars with other officers and our shift commander. At that time, I exited the car and the Lord impressed upon me to take off my gun belt which we were taught in the police academy never to do. I took off the gun belt and my hat and locked them in the trunk of the car and tried to present a non-threatening image to the man on the bridge. As I approached the man who was now on the outer edge of the bridge rail I said, "You don't want to jump". He asked "Why?" I answered, "Because God loves you and so do I". At that point, he asked me to repeat what I had said, which I did. To my astonishment, he then asked me, "Is your name John?". We conversed for a few minutes and God used me to talk him off the bridge. My lieutenant then turned him over to me and I took him to get help. On the way there, we talked and it came to mind that a week earlier on a day shift, I shared the gospel in a restaurant with a lady who was having some marital difficulties. I had encouraged her to see a pastor for counsel and to read the gospel of John, because God loved her and had an answer for her and her husband. It turned out that she was the wife of the man on the bridge, and she told him about the police officer who told her of the mercy and goodness of God. I was able to pray with the man because of the way God arranged the circumstances. He did not pray a prayer of salvation then, but I'm sure I planted good seeds in his life as I shared a hot meal and the love of God with him. We can all plant seeds of mercy and grace in the lives of others if we are willing to speak for Him. It may not feel comfortable at first, but remember, live by principles, not by feelings. Be faithful and stay on course. It's worth it a thousand times over!

Remember:
1. Stay on course.
2. Be honest.
3. God wants to heal your wounds.
4. Live by principles, not by feelings.
5. God will arrange circumstances.

CHAPTER THREE

KNOWING WHO YOU ARE IN CHRIST

Knowing who you are in Christ through the precious promises in His Word is the foundational place to start with any relationship, with any marriage, and especially in a blended family. The majority of widowed and divorced people do not take a season of their lives to deal with the magnitude of what they have been through. Pointing fingers and putting blame on others is not only unrealistic, but it short-changes your opportunity to evaluate your own responsibilities and actions in the previous marriage and thus, your opportunity to begin healing from your past. This is necessary in order to grow and change into a more Christ-like image, able to give yourself and your family the opportunity to fulfill the great purpose, destiny and promise the Lord has for each of you. By submitting to a season of healing, you can begin to realize who God says you are and what He will do in your life. You are beautifully and wonderfully made according to His Word (Psalm 139:14). You are the head and not the tail (Deuteronomy 28:13). God has good plans for you.

Ladies, the Lord did not create you to be a continual victim of abuse, neglect or rejection. These tragic behaviors continue to escalate in our society, even in church circles, and unfortunately, many of us did not take the time to heal from the wounds of this kind of behavior. We felt rejected, abused, lonely, and even though we had heard of the love of God, we still put up the walls. Some of us soon turned to dating or even a new spouse hoping that someone would fill the void. Remember, God promises that even the most desolate and unfortunate life will become productive and successful with His power. When problems from the past hold us captive today, we can hold onto the promise that the love of God will come again to refresh us and free us from the past. We can look to God for strength, wisdom acceptance and greatness and a new attitude toward the future. Even the end of the world will be a new beginning! God says "Behold, I will make all things new" (II Corinthians 5:17; Revelation 21:5).

Finding out who you are in Christ will take time and effort, the willingness to place yourself in a loving church environment, and the openness to receive teaching from the Bible on living by faith, not feelings. However, no amount of counseling or help from others will do any good unless you place yourself in the hands of the One Who created you. Yield yourself to His will, admitting where you are, and move ahead from there.

I have chosen to discuss several examples of the most common feelings of rejection and abuse that many experience through divorce. We will look at several scriptural examples of how Jesus Christ ministered life – not death; ministered healing – not hurt; ministered forgiveness – not bondage, releasing people from their past and opening the door to their future. Don't hold yourself hostage to the past through unforgiveness.

Many today treat women and children abusively. The definition of abuse is "misuse; mistreat; to put away from; to hurt by treating badly; to use insulting, course or bad language; to talk about; to scold harshly; to revile; to deceive wrongly; to injure; excessive use; a bad, unjust or corrupt custom or practice", according to Webster's dictionary. Abuse comes in many forms – physical, emotional, psychological and sexual. My years as a policeman and as a minister have taught me that this is a common attitude many males have toward their wives and children even in the church world. Many males still have selfish desires for their wives and getting their own needs met, not caring about the feelings of their wives. They demonstrate this by talking down to their wives, by intimidating them and by using fear against them. This attitude shows a selfishly motivated male, even though he may say he is committed to the Lord. Such an individual needs to humble himself before the Lord and ask his wife, and whoever else he has hurt, for forgiveness. There are also women who intimidate and manipulate to get their own way, and if this describes you, you need to follow the same pattern.

If you have lived with abuse, you've gone through pain and suffering that few know about. You've shed tears many a night and only the Lord knows the exact number of tears that have dripped down your face, even the silent tears in a church service or at a social gathering. You had a smile on your face but your heart was crushed and bruised. You, at times, had no feeling in your heart. You've said to yourself, "If this is what life is all about, I don't want to be part of it any more". You take care of everybody else's needs. You go through the motions and wonder who will care for you. Where is the comfort and tender touch that you need? Sometimes you feel like a dust cloth that serves the needs of others and then is put back on the shelf only to be taken down and used again another day. You are not alone. Remember, there are some needs in life, by design, that only God can meet for all of us. This does not take away the need for care and affection from a loving spouse and family, but begin to open up and ask God to show you who you are in His eyes. When you begin to realize that you are of infinite value and importance, and that every detail of your life matters to God, you will begin to receive strength and healing and a sense of purpose that will not only help you overcome your past, but will propel you into a meaningful future. No more if, maybe or possibly. You are God's own son or daughter, purchased with the ultimate price and your life is of the utmost importance to Him. He has a good plan for you. Never again will you allow yourself to be treated like a nobody, nor will you treat yourself that way. Live by a Godly standard and continually conform your ways to His. Respect yourself and expect others to respect you too.

You felt the pain of rejection. The males in your life did not touch you with loving care and compassion, but only for self-gratification. However, the man Jesus wants to come into your situation right now, as you read this. Allow Him to touch your heart and your mind compassionately. There are men, and your husband should be one of them, willing to become more Christ-like, to be your provider, your protector and your shelter. He can be these things to you as he relies on God's strength to help him. But remember, there are circumstances in life which leave voids in us that only God can fill.

The two women we will look at in the scripture have never been touched by a real man, only by selfish males. Now they are going to have an encounter with a real man, the man Christ Jesus. The woman who was caught in adultery was taken to Jesus and thrown down in the dirt by the religious males of the day (John 8). As stated before, this same attitude is detectable today in jokes, innuendoes and unhealthy attitudes, even in the church. This woman was a victim of her circumstances, not unlike many today who did not choose to be caught in their situations, abandoned, often with children and many responsibilities. She had no one to provide for her or to protect her. If this describes you, remember that you are still a lady created in the image of God, and the man Christ Jesus wants to make you whole. Start by asking Him for forgiveness and healing and do not dwell on the past. The emotional walls you have, the feelings of rejection or abuse, will heal as you put them down and begin picking up the thousands of promises God has for you. By finding these promises and speaking them to yourself, reading them daily, you will build your faith and your ability to go on. Put them on the refrigerator, put them in your Bible, in books, at your workplace, but most of all, put them in your mind, your mouth and in your heart. Constantly remind yourself that no weapon formed against you shall prosper, for example, and that you were made to be loved and cared for, protected from harm (Isaiah 54:17).

The Pharisee leaders did not show this woman compassion or the dignity she deserved; yes, dignity. Even though she was caught in the act of adultery, she was still made in the image of God, yet never touched by a real man. That dignity was still in her being because God created her. Instead of ministering life to her, the Pharisees had ulterior motives, wanting to trap Jesus in an error, so they used her for their purpose. They committed the same sin as the adulterous man who used her for his purpose.

I ask all males to become real men. If you are a Godly man reading this, then I say instruct, encourage, teach, even rebuke pharasaical men in your sphere of influence. Don't participate in the attitudes of our culture that demean women. Step up to the plate. Show respect to all women, treating them with dignity. Jesus knelt down and wrote in the sand, and I've heard many people speculate about what He wrote. Whatever it was, the men became ashamed and left. He said, "Let him who has not sinned cast the first stone". I believe those words touched those individuals around her, and since they knew they had sinned, they could not cast a stone. I believe Jesus wrote something especially for her in the dirt. Yes, God will take time and write in your heart that you are beautifully and wonderfully made, that you are a blossoming rose with a heavenly perfume, a sweet savor that can not be bought with any amount of gold on earth. The cost of this perfume was the precious blood of His Son, a free gift to you. As you fill yourself with His precious Word, the aroma of God's beauty will be evident in your life. His light will shine on your face. Then you will not look to your past but will walk in grace for today and hope for tomorrow. You will also be able to minister life to those around you who are in need.

Then Jesus said to the adulterous woman, "Go and sin no more. I do not condemn you". Jesus, the man who died on the cross, does not condemn you, so do not condemn yourself. Forgive those who have hurt you. As you forgive others, God will forgive you (Matthew 6:15). Realize that God has set you free from old ways and given you the opportunity to start clean and fresh. Decide to develop a spirit of praise and thanksgiving when you get up, when you go to work, when you go to sleep at night. This is critical to rising above your circumstances. Wherever you are, learn to give thanks and praise for God's will and work in your life. The woman caught in adultery, feeling rejected and hurt, certainly fit the description "abused".

Let's take a look at the Samaritan woman at the well (John 4:6-29). She, too, had been rejected by many males in her life and by the women of her town, as well. Women, remember her and don't reject your sisters around you. I don't mean natural-born sisters, but other women in the faith, women in church, at work or in your sphere of influence who are also trying to find their way to healing. Don't become jealous of them. Don't gossip about them, but be used by God as a healing force. Only you can make that choice. Even when you go through difficulties and are hurting yourself, if you give God's love and compassion to others, He will continue to heal the area of your life that is so in need.

According to Webster, the word reject means "not to accept; to hurt; to throw away or fling back; to refuse to take in; to refuse to agree to; to refuse to believe; to discard or throw away; worthless; cast off; cast out". Anyone who has been through a divorce, including children, goes through this emotional state of rejection. However, this does not have to be the end; it can be the beginning. All things become new when you come into relationship with the Lord and decide to plug into truth and His great purpose for you. As stated, the Samaritan woman at the well had been rejected repeatedly and was outcast, even among the women of her town. She, too, had been touched by many males but never by a true man. She is about to encounter Jesus the Christ. She was alone, about to draw water, one of the common chores of her day. In her culture and time, women usually went to draw water in groups for safety and company at particular times of the day. She was not welcome with the other women so she went alone. What an opportunity Jesus found there. She was alone. You know, even if you manage a home and family, belong to a church, go out to work each day, you may still feel very much alone. That's okay. Sometimes it's a good place to be to encounter Jesus. Jesus talked to her. He will talk to you too. In fact, He has written you a love letter in the form of His Word. In this letter, He tells you much about your destiny and purpose. He tells you how to walk in His blessing. He tells you that you are gifted and important in the scheme of things (Romans 12:6-11). Yes, this is a recurring theme in this book because I have seen our streets, our counseling centers, our church offices filled with people who are abused and rejected with no knowledge of who they are in God. He wants to manifest Himself to you and through you. This can be a new day for you and for anyone willing to encounter the real Jesus.

This woman at the well did not refuse to talk to the Lord. You, too, must spend time with Him, taking in His Word, enjoying the love letter He has written you, speaking to Him aloud. Communicate with Him daily. What did Jesus say to her that changed her life? He told her that if she knew the gift God had for her, the living water, she would never thirst again. He, of course, spoke of Himself. An interesting conversation developed between them. They discussed how and where to worship, and Jesus told her we must worship the Father in spirit and truth. This true worship will take anyone from rejection and loneliness to the living well. He also spoke the truth to her in love. He said that she had five husbands and the man she now had was not her husband. She received His words. It's sometimes difficult to hear the truth, but she did not become offended or aloof. Jesus wanted her to deal with her past so He could put it far from her and never bring it up to her again. Once we confess to the Lord, we are told He forgives our sins and puts them "as far as the east is from the west" (Psalm 103:12). She was freed! The woman was able to go on from there and tell others of the great gift she received from the man at the well. He still gives living water today. His promises are to all who come into relationship with Him. Men and women, rise up with your spouse and your family and determine to go God's way. Speak kindness to one another. Forgive one another. Encourage one another. Determine to bless, not to curse; to build up rather than tear down. Be channels of mercy and living water.

Faith vs. Feeling

As a police officer, when I would ask someone why he or she did something, countless times I heard, "Because I felt like it". That's a very poor excuse to hurt others. There may be many times when we feel like quitting or like saying hurtful words to each other. We may feel like life will never get any better, but we should not be ruled by our feelings. After my injury in 1981, we watched my body, my mind and my personality change over a period of months, changes that would last many years. I went through many medical tests after which I would come home feeling dirty and violated. During that period of my life, I took many showers trying to feel clean. I was also forced to go through the legal system in regard to my "performance of duty disability". Neither of these systems was very friendly and I understand that. Although a victim of this accident, I was made to feel that I was the cause of it. The taking of excessive showers, for example, was a way of trying to cleanse myself of the filth and the guilt feelings which others tried to place on me. However, the Lord is faithful, and over a number of years, has healed me from this aspect of the injury. I understand how many of you have been made to feel that it is your fault you have been rejected or abandoned. This is not the truth. Don't believe the lie. God will heal you too from the guilt or guilt feelings you have taken on in the past. As you accept this, your behavior will change accordingly. You must begin to tell yourself, "It's not my fault when things go wrong. I am not responsible for every problem. I will deal with problems, but I am not the cause of every problem".

The injury to my nervous system caused chemical imbalances in my body to put me on an emotional roller coaster. Like a woman in a monthly cycle or change of life, people who have been exposed to toxic chemicals experience these highs and lows. I would cry for no apparent reason, or drive up to a store and seeing several cars, become fearful of being around people and drive back home without going in. I would push my wife and family away from me, wanting to be alone all the time. However, deep inside I did not want to be alone. Just like others who go through these emotional cycles, I didn't want to cry uncontrollably or go through mood swings. I understand what it's like because I, too, had to get a handle on my feelings. I used to be an observer of this behavior, but now I have lived through emotional upheaval and the deepest despair. Thank God, He has brought me and my family out of this dark season, and He will do it for you, too.

Let's define "feel" and "feelings" and then discover how to replace the feelings with faith. Webster says that feel means "to perceive or be aware of; to be influenced by;

to be sensitive to or be emotionally disturbed by". Feeling means "awareness; consciousness; emotion; sensitivity; passion; sentiment or premonition". Until the deeper ties are created in your new family, it is not unusual to feel somewhat disconnected from everyone. You may feel that you are not really being touched by anyone. Sometimes we develop an unhealthy attitude that no one cares because we "feel" we are not really connecting with people the way we should. At those times, we have to dig ourselves out of the pit, as I found myself doing at the lowest point after my injury. I had repeated nightmares, eating disorders, temper flares and emotional outbursts, anger and unforgiveness. I loved the Lord and served Him previous to this, but coupled with the pressures of a new family, I had a lot to deal with. I still had to choose Christ's attitude. I was instructed to see many physicians, and I have documentation stating that it was my faith in the Lord and His Word that kept me from suicide. It was faith that enabled me to maintain an attitude of going forward in life and also helping others in need. This is proof that, in any season of your life, choosing the Lord's way according to His Word will enable you to go through the valleys and overcome great obstacles.

God will not leave you; His love for you is a fact. You are not to base your attitude toward life on how you feel about yourself, others or your circumstances. Your worth is not based upon how pretty or handsome you are, how much money you have, how strong you are or on your titles or ministry. None of these things determines God's love for you or how much He values you. He loves you unconditionally. No matter what you feel like, He will never stop loving you or cut you off from His promises. His desire for you is abundant life as you walk in the newness of His Word (John 10:10). That is why forgiveness of yourself and others is critical to the blended family. Put off the old, put on the new.

I did not know the Lord when I was divorced and had no knowledge of His love, forgiveness or character in the person of Jesus Christ. The only answer I saw and the only counsel I was given was to divorce. I know the tremendous heartache, rejection, pain and mistrust that develop when a marriage breaks up. I know the suffering you have endured because I have been there too. My infant daughter was six months old when the divorce was final. The rejection and hurt I felt turned into anger, bitterness and unforgiveness. As a police officer, I vented that anger at work for a short season, but I soon determined that I would not allow those feelings to dictate my future. I put off the old and put on the new.

I learned much from my wife's experience of healing from her first marriage in which alcohol abuse played a part. What she did is what most of us have not done. She spent years as a single parent, content to let God be her husband and provider. She learned to be the loving, caring, compassionate wife she is to me by learning to live the Lord's way in those years she was single. That is the best option. However, start where you are today. Start with forgiveness from Christ. Forgive those around you and determine to walk a higher road. Don't base your future and your family's future on the emotional leftovers of the past.

Once I came to the Lord, I began to replace the negative feelings with thoughts about who God says I am, and handled the hurt and rejection the way the Bible said to handle it. I gave it up and let God renew me, and I have never regretted anything I let go. He is gracious and merciful, and will replace anything you give Him with acceptance and a new self-image. He wants to break the cycle of divorce which is in many families. I had the unfortunate distinction of being the first in my family to be divorced, so I felt a lot of guilt and condemnation because of that. But God has replaced all pain and emotional upheaval of the divorce and the injury with wholeness and wellness. He wants to do the same for you. He loves you and you can receive that love by faith right now. Thank Him for it. You and your family can have many great years ahead. You have the opportunity to start a new chapter, a new book. You can even relate to your former spouse with no bitterness or resentment. My wife and I have experienced friendly communication in these relationships for years now, and so can you. Not only is it possible, but it's worth the effort. Learn who God says you are and what He will help you do. He is the God of new beginnings.

Remember:
1. Take time to see yourself as God sees you.
2. You are of infinite value.
3. Only God can meet some of your needs.
4. Forgive.
5. Live by faith, not by feelings.

CHAPTER FOUR

INTIMACY WITH GOD, YOURSELF AND YOUR SPOUSE

If we ask the majority of men, even Christian men, the question "What is intimacy?", they immediately think of the physical union between a husband and wife. This concept of sexual relations is one that our nation, as a whole, is constantly bombarded with from commercials to sporting events. No matter what product is being sold over the airwaves, there is always the suggestion that love equals sex. As stated before, sex is a part of the marriage relationship, but we feel it equals love because we don't know our whole purpose in life. We can only discover that purpose through intimacy with our Creator. We men, especially, need to learn that if we do not open ourselves up to God, we will never become truly intimate with our wives. To define the word intimate, Webster lists these shades of meaning: close; acquaintance; familiarity with; sharing one's innermost being; informative and private; very personal. True intimacy encompasses all these and carries forward to include sexual relationship in marriage.

In Genesis 3:10, the Lord God called out to Adam "Where are you?" and Adam answered, "I heard your voice in the garden and I was afraid because I was naked, and I hid myself". What Adam was saying was, "I didn't want you to know what I was doing, how I was feeling and what I was thinking". Thus he started the chain reaction of men running from God. It wasn't until the Lord Jesus Christ completed his earthly ministry, death and resurrection that we were able to stop running. He not only has given us the opportunity and power to stop running and hiding from God, but He empowers us to run TO HIM instead. As we learn to open our inner selves to God, we will get to know ourselves better and be changed into the men God wants us to be. There is healing and safety in being open and vulnerable to God, and in doing so, we learn to become more open with those around us. This is, of course, true for women too, but it is generally agreed that men have more difficulty being open and expressive.

Let me talk about several steps to help men accomplish a greater depth of intimacy. Both men and women are the bride of Christ. However, we men don't know what it means to be a bride! We understand being a groom, but what is it like to be a bride? What does a bride feel? What does a bride expect and what is expected of her? As we understand better the relationship between Christ and His bride, we will see another dimension of relationship that is possible with our wives.

We have all been guests at weddings at some time or other, watching the bride walk down the aisle. I don't know about you but I've never seen a bride that wasn't beautiful. However, the bride walking down the aisle is the product of many months, maybe even years of planning and preparing. Every detail is planned and executed with precision. She is standing there in a beautiful dress, every hair and eyelash is in place and her make-up is perfect. There is music in the background creating the mood and flowers adorn the setting. The air is filled with the expectancy of a joyous occasion and well it should be. But the atmosphere wasn't created in just a few moments. If we can understand this, we can blend that understanding into our relationships with our wives and create an atmosphere of intimacy that will pervade every room in the house. The bride carefully plans every detail of her coming wedding. Men, you might think that much of this detail work is foolish, but it isn't. The detailed planning of the bride is not unlike what Christ expects of us in relationship to Him. She prepares, she waits, she expects, she saves herself for her husband. A bride surrenders herself body, soul and spirit at the altar, giving her innermost self to her bridegroom and relinquishing her "self". She expects to be embraced with tenderness, to be complemented on her beauty and told how much she is loved and needed by him. She expects to be protected and to be the only one he shares his heart with from now on.

You see, the Lord expects us to be preparing ourselves for His purposes, to be patient and wait on Him, to be faithful to Him, to save ourselves for Him and to please Him. Just as the bride surrenders herself completely at the altar, the Lord Jesus expects us to humble our hearts, our attitudes, our minds and our bodies. As we humble ourselves and take on His lifestyle, we can expect the Lord to embrace us as men, to show us compassion and tenderness. He has written the Bible as a letter to us to say that He loves us and that He has sent His son to die for us. As we allow this to sink into our being and comprehend it slowly, our character and focus will change accordingly, allowing intimacy to develop. Spiritual affection will be born out of this knowledge and time spent in His presence and His Word. After all, can you have a marriage without affection? We begin to realize that we love Him because He loved us first (John 4:19).

We can apply the same principle in our relationship with our wives. This willingness to let someone else inside is the open door to the trust that makes relationships grow. It is in accepting one another and sharing your innermost thoughts, needs, goals and dreams that you will bond deeply with each other. Taking time to be together, to listen to one another and enjoy each other's company will help you to get to know each other better, no matter how long you've been together. Praying for each other's needs and concerns, and confessing your faults will keep you humble and bring healing (James 5:16). Intimacy develops as you are willing to be vulnerable, and allow yourself and your spouse to make mistakes. Remember that you are a team, on the same side, facing life together. Meet every crisis with mutual trust and respect, and you will learn to be each other's greatest friend and supporter. Share each other's sense of humor and, by all means, learn to laugh at yourself. You should feel the need to be with each other as well as to have time alone. You will create this intimacy out of a loving, wanting heart and you accomplish it by humbling yourself. Learning to be open and "real" with God will prepare you to be open and genuine with your spouse.

Right now, even if you have a relationship with the Lord, all you have to do is say, "Father God, help me...". You may have walked down the aisle of a church in response to an altar call, or prayed a prayer, yet not wholly committed yourself and your future to Him. I sometimes liken that walk down the aisle to the marriage ceremony. Take the opportunity to make an altar right now wherever you are and say, "Father God, I'm asking You to retool my heart into the image of Your Son's heart, full of compassion, love and integrity. Equip me as never before". Praying that prayer and then following through as God enables you will help you develop a lifestyle of intimacy between you and your Savior, you and your wife, and you and your family. This process may be costly. It may mean some planing on the sharp edges and sanding off of rough places. The Master Carpenter knows exactly what we need to prepare and equip us for life. This process is painful but necessary, and often, we do not know what is going on inside of us. We may shed tears as old, familiar things are uprooted and, if you read the Bible, you know that real men do cry. I have been through seasons of my life when I could not cry, and I wanted to. But through the Lord's mercy and tenderness and the healing patience of a loving wife, I am able to shed tears again.

I encourage you to welcome the pain of retooling. It's important to empty yourself out so that God can replace some things in you. How do you do that? Start by taking a walk every day. This will accomplish several things. It will give you better physical health and more energy for starters. As you walk, simply talk to God out loud. As you empty yourself out, you have more capacity to receive His goodness, tenderness, wisdom and direction for you and your family. Another simple measure is getting up earlier in the morning to spend time in the scripture over your coffee. Let God search the depths of your being and be honest about what comes up. You can also listen to the Word or sound Bible teaching on tape as you go to and from work. These are ways of cooperating with the Carpenter as He works His design in you. By being faithful to these few simple things, you will feel better physically as you reduce the stress in your life, and spiritually as you take in the Word and the presence of God. This intimacy is life-changing (Isaiah 64:8).

Another important aspect of becoming a man of intimacy and integrity is a commitment to a local church. God will make many changes in your life through fellow believers and a praying support system. (See Chapter 11)

Ladies, I encourage you to allow your husbands to make mistakes. For example, if he has made a decision to come closer to the Lord, allow him to be imperfect as he grows without constant correction from you. Remember, as you trust the Lord, He will not allow anything to hurt you. By being an encouragement to your husband and also by creating an atmosphere for intimacy in your home, he will feel the freedom to grow without feeling pressured to be perfect.

The Bullet-Proof Vest

This atmosphere should be created by both spouses. We all have times when we can take the lead in this respect, providing for special times together. Wives can arrange for the children to go to a friend's house, for example, while making his favorite dinner. Wear his favorite perfume and a dress he especially likes. Offer a back rub or something that will relax him. Make ordinary times extraordinary in simple, inexpensive ways. One example of my wife's expression of love for me goes back to when I worked as a police officer. I was one of the first officers in our area to wear a bullet-proof vest and there were occasions when the vest protected my life. I began to notice that men wear "vests" that keep things from touching them. I'm referring to things like conversation with their wives. Because I loved and trusted my wife and knew she wouldn't harm me, I would come home from work and "take off my vest". She would offer me a cup of tea and a foot massage or something equally relaxing and allow me to put my guard down, so to speak. I would sit with her after work and talk for hours. These times enabled us to know each other's thoughts, feelings and circumstances. They were wonderful times when we came to know each other deeply and I grew in my ability to be open.

Make some time for your husband to "take off his vest", to feel free to express himself, and he will learn to be more open. Then protect him. He is making himself vulnerable by sharing his inner heart. Nothing will squelch this kind of intimacy faster than knowing that what is shared between you does not stay between you. Do not repeat or make light of anything that is shared in your close moments if you value the development of your relationship. Protect each other's inner heart and ability to be open and honest.

Men, you have to be the one to "take off the vest", so start right now by sharing your thoughts, needs and desires with your wife. Give her opportunity to encourage you and to pray together with you. As you do this, you will sense a binding together and a deeper trust that will cause your family to grow and prosper.

Expressing Love

How do we show love to our wives? What is it that they are looking for? Do they want us to work all the time to provide? Providing is an important part of loving your wife and family, but there are some even greater desires and needs that money cannot fulfill. She needs you to spend time with her and share yourself from the heart. Do not use fear and intimidation as you talk to your wife and children. They take our words to heart. Use the simple basic courtesy of saying "Please" and Thank you", "Would you please do this?" and "I appreciate that you did thus and so". Don't forget the ever so important "I'm sorry. I made a mistake". It's important for the husband and father to ask forgiveness when necessary, important for the moment and for the investment in the future. Build bridges of communication with all family members. As you speak humbly and politely to each other, you will begin to put down some of the walls in your life. You and your family will find that communication is safe. Don't expect the children to come to you and talk when they have problems if you give the impression that you are unapproachable. There will be times when you will have to force yourself to talk about how you are feeling or what you are experiencing. I know the difficulty of not wanting to talk to anyone, yet needing to desperately. However, as you determine to put down your walls, the family will gain a cohesiveness and a sense of love and acceptance. The demonstration of loving your wife will have a powerful effect on your children, and the older ones will see first-hand that we all need to change and can learn to accommodate each other's needs. Sending your wife cards, notes, letters, and flowers are small in terms of cost, but they are not small things in her eyes. By depositing into her life a sense of her worth, her greatness and her value to you, you are letting her know that she is the only woman who can fill that most important place in your life. Understand that there are certain areas of need in both husband and wife that only God can fill and we are this way by design. We must remember this so that we do not put unrealistic expectations on our spouses. Let's realize that as we ourselves change, we affect the willingness of those around us to change as well.

Husbands can provide for special times together, too. This can be anything from a walk in the park and a rented movie to a night out at a favorite restaurant. This does not have to be an expensive affair that will add financial pressure. All she wants is for you to take time for her, to care enough to do the special "little" things that say "I love you". Learn to put her needs first and then she can help you and the children grow and prosper as she is more fulfilled and secure in your love. As the children see you love their mother and protect and care for her, they will learn how a Godly man is to act toward women, how to treat them with respect and dignity. Thus, you can be used to break the cycle of divorce from the root by teaching and demonstrating the relationship skills that make for a strong marriage. May I encourage you now to say, "Lord, I am submitting to Your Word and by the blood of Christ, we are breaking the cycle of divorce in this family". You can start placing your family under the blessing of the Lord right now, no matter what the past. Also, as your sons see this, they will learn how to properly interact with a wife and not be selfishly motivated in their treatment of their own wives. This will also be a gauge for your daughters as they will want to marry a man who treats them like Dad treats Mom. They will look for a man who, like Dad, takes on the attributes of the heavenly Father. Don't underestimate the power of your example.

Another aspect of unspoken communication is the father's investment of time in the children. This speaks silently to your wife, and to the children themselves, that they are important and that this marriage and family will grow and stay together through all seasons of life. Take your sons out in the woods or to ball games, as well as taking them to church and to serve others so they can see that a Godly life is a balanced life. Take your daughters out on "dates" as I still do with mine. We must deposit into our children examples of how Godly people live and treat one another so that they can also make good choices.

Another way of increasing intimate communication with your wife is by taking responsibility for spiritual headship. This does not have to be a great inner struggle either. Ask the Lord and your wife for help. Be a part of a men's fellowship or discipleship group, too. Spend time with the children reading the Word and just discussing life issues from the Biblical perspective. This does not always have to be in a formal setting, but just during your usual activities. As you grow in integrity and character, this will filter to your children. Your wife will want to follow your leadership. It will not be a case of "have to" but "want to" as she sees you change and grow. All family members will learn the importance of intimacy to lasting relationships, and can appropriate by your example the skills that will make them better marriage partners.

Listening, Loving and Laughing

May I encourage wives who may have had poor relationships in marriage before that you can learn all over again, or maybe for the first time, how to speak and listen on a deeper level. Listen by looking into your husband's heart with the eyes of the Lord, not fault-finding, demeaning or being disrespectful. This is extremely important whether at home or in the company of others. Listening with the heart of Christ is having compassion, understanding and the ability to see your husband as God sees him – the finished product. See him as a man yielded to God, a man of integrity, compassion and honesty; one who will put you and your family ahead of his own needs (and desires at times). Be a woman of prayer and speak aloud right now the goodness of God in your life. Speaking words of encouragement and faith to your husband, will help him rediscover his courage and leadership in spite of past failure. Choose to be that woman who encourages her husband not to quit, but to keep on striving for better, more meaningful relationship.

When my wife Lee and I first married, my actions, attitudes and character were not always those of a Godly man. Not being fully healed emotionally, the events of my past still influenced me and clouded my decisions. In addition, the injury I suffered left me with physical, mental and emotional impairments. It was so severe that the doctors didn't even fully understand the nature of the injury or the complications that could arise because of it. During this time, my wife still created an atmosphere of intimacy, depositing in me her healing words. She would write me notes, leave Bible verses for me to read and encourage me about the future. She allowed me to fail. She did not act superior to me or challenge me in any way, even at times when I could not walk or talk properly or engage in the normal activities I enjoyed before the accident. She saw me through the emotional flare-ups and temper outbursts when my brain literally could not handle the stresses of day-to-day life. These outbursts were often directed at our sons in the form of verbal abuse, lack of patience and even physical roughness at times. All this did not stop her from loving me to wholeness. It was the love of God through her that, for many years, kept me above the line where I knew there was hope and healing for me. Her guidance and support were critical to my healing. There were days when I would not talk to her, being totally shut in. She continued to love me even though I sometimes pushed her away and told her I did not want her around. She persisted, crying many tears in private. She saw me change from a man full of strength and capacity to one who could not go to work or handle the pressures of daily life. Yet, there were times when she had to confront me with issues, especially the treatment of our sons. But she did this in a manner that was not threatening or belittling to me. She let me know I had to deal with the issue. As I faced this, allowing the Lord to make changes in me, I started out on the road to recovery. This is one example of how a spouse can create an atmosphere of intimacy that goes far beyond physical romance regardless of the obstacles. This type of intimacy in a marriage shows a great degree of love and commitment and the true ability we have to love one another out of the love of God in us.

This was a great example to our family and also helped many to whom we have ministered over the years to understand that God would not let them down regardless of what difficulty they were facing. His grace, His wisdom, His mercy and even His joy could be experienced at all times. There was still peace and joy in our home during the years of great struggle with my injury. I was not able to relax with laughter and joking for some time, but eventually that came around too. As I stated before, it was my wife's Christ-like love that kept me on track and gave me a contentment and an ability to enjoy life even during great trial. Husbands and wives, encourage one another and you will create loving, understanding and lasting relationships.

Let Old Things Die

The marriage altar is a place of new beginnings. Every couple must deal with the past so it can truly by put behind. As you get to know one another better in heart and spirit, you will gain a greater appreciation for the physical union as well. We have ministered to couples who have brought up their past relationships to each other with regard to physical romance. These individuals would compare spouses in times of anger or stress, saying hurtful things. They would hold onto cards, notes, pictures or other inappropriate memorabilia that simply should be forgotten about at the new marriage altar. Don't be guilty of these destructive behaviors. We encourage you in the place of new beginnings to make a complete fresh start, treating each other with respect and dignity. And men, don't carry the worldly attitudes about sexual relationships into your home. Treat your wife with a higher level of dignity. As you gain a greater perspective of manhood under the Lord, you will find that many of the attitudes and tastes of our culture simply are not edifying to womanhood. Take a stand as a true man of God and show great concern for your wife in this area. Don't allow the worldly attitudes to survive here. You may have daughters, living with you or not, to whom your attitudes toward women will filter down. Deposit in your wife what is for her best and her wholeness as a great lady, and you will affect your daughter's life also.

This is a great opportunity to start a fresh life, learning from our past but not allowing it to dictate our future. Build each other up. Men, become your wife's protector and friend as well. Allow her to talk openly and to express her concerns and feelings about matters. Her feelings and her point of view may be different, but we're designed to be complementary – to balance each other, to learn from each other and to draw strength from each other. Don't allow your wife's feelings, which you may not understand, to cloud your view of her. By allowing her to express herself, you help her to become the woman God created her to be. Then learn from the differences and from her point of view. Due to my past, I had a very difficult time accomplishing this simply because I viewed my wife as the enemy every time she had a different perspective on any particular subject. However, as I experienced healing and became more open to her, I saw that her differences were my strengths. So I encourage you to allow your wife to be herself, to share her inmost being with you. You can also learn to be more open and expressive from her. After all, intimacy is knowing each other better, being able to be ourselves, and developing a deeper love and trust.

Women, show confidence in your husband's leadership ability and he will grow to fulfill your expectations.

Remember:
1. It is God's desire to have an intimate relationship with you.
2. Take off the vest and protect each other's confidences.
3. Be courteous to each other.
4. Provide for special times together.
5. Let old things die.

CHAPTER FIVE

COMMUNICATION IN MARRIAGE

God has created us with the ability to communicate powerfully with words and actions. The Bible has a great deal to say about communication, and volumes have been written on everything from listening skills to body language. It is not my purpose to rewrite those things here, but rather to look at some attitudes behind how we communicate.

Most married couples have difficulty, at times, communicating with one another and can learn to make improvements. The challenge in the blended family is to learn not to filter all communication through your past pain and rejection. It is critical to leave the past behind and to determine that your self-image will be shaped by God's Word. You will communicate what is in your heart – for better or for worse! Let the abundance of your heart be life changing. Remember, change comes from the renewing of the mind (Romans 12:2). You can bring peace and change to your family by strengthening these four areas:

1 – The Golden Rule

The Golden Rule, of course, means treating your spouse the way you want to be treated (Luke 6:31). When you truly give respect, dignity and honesty, you encourage "teachability" and receptivity in each other. The husband should take the lead here and, as the scripture says so often, humble himself before the Lord. This refers to the simple admission that you and I can not handle all the responsibilities of husband, father and breadwinner, so we invite the Lord into all aspects of our lives, not just Sunday morning. We are humbling ourselves by continuing to put down our walls, and then by asking our wives to join us in inviting the Lord to be the center of our marriage and family. As you discuss this with your wife, look into her eyes, take her hand and say a simple prayer with her like, "Lord, help us." This prayer coupled with a heart willing to change will bring the Lord's strength into your marriage like never before. A wife may also pray this simple prayer if her husband is not yet taking the lead.

Becoming teachable helps us recognize each other's strengths and weaknesses. Due to my injury, I had a difficult time with this when Lee and I first married. As I stated before, I viewed her as the enemy in every disagreement. It took a season of my life to recognize that, even when we disagreed, she was truly on my side. Once I believed that we were on the same team, I was able to receive from her many strengths and talents. By putting my strengths together with hers, we learned to harmonize as we were intended to. We see our differences as positive, not negative, like weights that balance a scale. We've learned to see each other's perspective as important to every situation. We see life more fully by being open to each other's ideas.

Have family gatherings at the supper table and allow your children to share their experiences and feelings also. When they share suggestions, pray about them and give some feedback. Bringing the children into discussions will bring the family closer, and the children will recognize that they have value and that what they say is important to you. When you reach a decision on one of their suggestions, tell them why it could or could not be used. In either case, they will still have valuable input. Men, as you continue to become servant leaders, you will create an environment in which your wife can become more yielding to you. As a couple, you submit to each other lovingly. As your leadership develops and your wife sees that your decisions are for her best interest and that of the family, there will be fewer disagreements in the decision-making process.

When Lee and I married, she had a mature relationship with the Lord. She was a teacher of the Word on a regular basis, and pastors would call her for insight on various matters. Many people called upon her for counsel. It got to the point where this added to the rejection I felt due to the injury and I became angry. However, I did not allow this anger to be a negative force. I simply said, "Lord, Your Word states that I am to be the head of my wife – not a dictator, not a ruler, - but a servant leader. I'm asking You to teach me how to be that leader." I then went to my wife and explained the decision I made. Her greatest asset to me every day was her continual life style of great love and compassion, and the Godly wisdom she possessed. Talking was very difficult for me after the injury, but I knew I had to start there. The Lord gave me strength to take down my walls one block at a time. I could not read for many years, so I would listen to the Bible on tape and to various teaching tapes that would help me in the process of becoming a servant leader.

Do not let any obstacle in your path stop you from fulfilling your goal. Our goal was to have a loving family that was submitted to the will and the ways of God. Also, I wanted to become a whole person again, healed in every sense. There was much going on in my life then and at times, it appeared I was not attaining my goals. However, we can not judge by appearances or feelings. We judge by the written Word of God and by faith in the living Lord. As I was faithful, persistent and forgiving, God was more than faithful to equip me with the strength to be an overcomer.

Another aspect of "teachability" is becoming active in a local church (See Chapter 11). As you become open to teaching, you will also find avenues and outlets through which you can encourage others in their struggles.

Some ladies might say, "John, my husband won't take the proper headship of our home. He won't have anything to do with God or the church, but his only concern is for his own selfish desires, his own wants." You might say, "It's not fair", and you are absolutely correct. Life is not fair and there are seasons when women, through their willingness and closeness to the family, do set the spiritual tone in the home. Start where you are. Treat him the way you want him to treat you. If your husband does not want to participate and is closing the door, you need to ask the Lord for wisdom and strength. Go to him and let him know that even though he does not want to attend church, you will attend with the children every week. Let him know that you would like him to be involved, but if he chooses not to be, you will still follow the same course. First of all, be faithful to church services and time in the Word yourself. Go to a ladies' Bible study and have the children join youth activities. Always inform your husband of what is happening at church and invite him. Let him know he is always welcome and that at any point in time, you are willing to give him the place of spiritual responsibility. If he's not going to take that responsibility right now, you should. The Lord will bless your effort to bring your marriage into strength and longevity.

Be faithful and always be a loving support to your husband. Take interest in what he does on the job, for example. You will win him by love, not by nagging! He will notice the changes in you. When he sees you taking a course of strength, purpose and stability, and sees the things of the Lord "paying dividends", he may begin to respond. As you remain faithful and persistent, there will be a contentment in your whole being. Men can not resist this type of love for long. What you are doing is allowing the Lord to work on behalf of you and your family. Yes, you are standing in the gap for him just as, someday, he will stand in the gap for you. So be faithful and encouraged. Your persevering will produce a spirit of thanksgiving and contentment in you, and a desire for what you are experiencing in him. Look to the Lord to touch your husband's heart while you gain strength from hearing the Word regularly, from prayer and praise, and from spending time in the Bible yourself. Sow the seeds of love, patience and understanding that you want to harvest in the years ahead.

2 – Learn Positive Problem-solving Skills

We are all familiar with negative attitudes that do not solve problems like the "blame game". No matter what topic is discussed, we have the opportunity to pick apart our spouse's past, to blame each other, the children or past experiences for present problems. However, we don't have to operate in this attitude and we don't always have to be right! We can choose to take all obstacles that come our way and deal with them in a manner that is pleasing to God – no sarcasm, cold shoulder or manipulation. If the problem is in the area of finances, for example, we should discuss the various related issues and how we can achieve our financial goals. We might need to create a positive cash flow or get out of debt. If we blame each other and bring up hurtful things from the past, we are not being truthful and we are putting wedges between ourselves instead of building bridges. Again, sit with your spouse, discuss your goals and needs, and pray a simple prayer like, "Lord, we are turning to Your Word. What do you have to say about finances?" Are we tithing? Are we giving? Do we have a budget? Are we good stewards of what we already have? (See Chapter 7). As we determine to learn problem-solving skills, we will overcome obstacles that would have, otherwise, defeated us.

One way for a wife who is at home to help her husband in this area is to give him some time when he comes home from work to relax and unwind. Make his arrival time as pleasant as possible. By giving him a chance to unwind, eat dinner and be glad that he's home, he will be better able and ready to face issues when they need to be discussed. Letting him know in a gentle way that you need to discuss a problem later on is much more effective than bombarding him at the door with the day's troubles. Give him a chance to unload his pressures. Men, the same is true for your wives. They work all day in the home or outside of the home, coupled with the responsibilities of being a wife and mother, and they also need time to relax. So give each other this courtesy, and let your spouse know when you need time later on to discuss an issue so that he or she can be prepared, and emotions will not be running high. You might also occasionally agree to set a day and time to discuss a particular problem so that both of you can be prepared ahead of time. Be willing to learn new approaches so you can handle situations constructively. Remember, you are on the same team!

3 – Agreement

One of the most dynamic forces in relationships is the principle of agreement. This is true for every relationship in life but here we will limit the discussion to marriage. If you and I could only recognize that as we come into agreement, we have great power and no obstacle we face will be able to divide us. If you remember the story of the Tower of Babel (Genesis 11), God said that because the people could communicate and they were of one mind, they could accomplish anything they could imagine! Think about that.

Agreement is accomplished as a husband and wife learn to love and trust each other, and see themselves as one force with one goal and one destiny. This will help weld them together through the most difficult of times. Even when there is disagreement on a certain subject, if it is known that the husband has the highest good of his wife and family at heart, he can even be allowed to fail. No disastrous consequences will befall us as we trust each other, because our ultimate trust is in God to lead our families.

An important aspect of communicating in agreement is learning to listen well and discuss issues without arguing. Most of us need practice giving our undivided attention and permitting others to speak without interruption. As we develop our sense of being on the same team, we will not feel so threatened every time we differ on an issue. Our willingness to listen will also help our spouses to be better listeners because they will not have to compete to be heard. Try to make eye contact while talking and hold your emotions until you have had time to process what has been said. You can restate what has been said to be sure there is no miscommunication, and at least give a partial response and a sense that you are receiving what your partner is saying. Nothing will shut down meaningful communication quicker than feeling that what you have to say is not important to the hearer. Put down the newspaper, the book or the remote control and really LISTEN. It goes a long way toward intimacy. Even if you don't have an answer, if you listen to me, I know you care. Of course, a touch, a hug, a listening ear help me get things off my chest.

The last and most important point on agreement is to pray together. God can show you creative solutions and strategies you may not have considered, and it's difficult to be angry and humble at the same time! In discussing heated issues, we must always remember to attack the problems, not each other. I repeat, we are on the same team. Determine that your relationship is more important than any single issue, and don't allow anything to divide you.

These few guidelines will help enormously in solving problems because they are not only method changes but attitude changes that will help you see your spouse in a new light. My wife's trust and faith for provision, for example, is not first in me but in God. If I make a poor choice, we're not going to be devastated because God is still in control and we will learn and grow from our mistakes. We're in this together. I have also learned to listen to her input and carefully weigh her point of view. As we do this and measure our choices against God's Word, we diminish the possibility of disagreement. Even if we do disagree, our children need to see the unity between us, submitting to each other in love and letting the Biblical principles guide our choices. This keeps harmony in our relationship and an inseparable bond between us. Usually, problems do not arise overnight and solutions for success are not accomplished overnight. So take small bites of big problems, agree upon solutions, pray and take steps to reach your goals together. Agreement is accomplished by loving words, encouragement, humility, willingness to give your spouse the benefit of the doubt, and lovingly submitting ourselves to the Lord and to each other. This leaves little room for division between husband and wife, but much for growth, intimacy and learning wisdom.

4 – Learn to Affirm

Affirming or building up your spouse goes a long way in encouraging trust and openness. Never tear down, at home or in public. During the years I was severely damaged, my wife always affirmed me and my place as head of the family by her loving care, her touch, her gentleness and her trust. Yes, there were issues I had to deal with but she brought them to me in such a way that I could face them. As my wife would go through difficult seasons of her life, I would also take the opportunity to encourage her and build her up, to let her know that she is the most important woman in the world. Remind your spouse of the qualities in him or her that you appreciate and admire. Affirmation is really watering the seeds of intimacy. These are every day choices that we make for one another's good. As you love and affirm each other, you will find your trust growing, the atmosphere in your home changing and the communication between you becoming more meaningful and on a higher level. If you are going through a difficult time right now, remember the good qualities in your spouse that drew you to him or her in the first place, and encourage those. Words of praise and appreciation go a long, long way.

Attitude is Everything

I need to emphasize that we should not treat our spouses or our children as our enemies. We should not tell them, by our words or actions, that they are the causes of our frustration, disappointment, hurt or unhappiness. If we continue to do so, they will not see any hope for the future. What should we do when we feel frustrated, hurt and angry?

We should start by looking at ourselves. You heard correctly. Start with yourself. Place yourself under the forgiveness of the Lord, and ask Him to begin to change you, your attitude, your frustration. I did this many times and learned to channel the frustration of my injury to God's faithfulness. I took a lot of pressure off myself, my wife and my children by writing my thoughts and prayers in a notebook. I'd put the date and time on the page, often in the wee hours of the morning. (This is still helpful to me when I don't sleep well.) I would focus my writing on God's goodness and faithfulness. I could not read books back then so this was my way of "emptying out" – putting my prayers and concerns on paper. I'd ask the Lord to change me. This would relieve some frustration and stress, and enable me to change my attitude. I learned to speak to our children in a softer voice and with a proper manner. The violence in me eventually subsided as I committed myself to change. If you start with yourself, your spouse and children will see the difference in you, and see that change is possible for them also.

Another way of relieving stress and frustration is physical exercise, if you are able to do some. For about twelve years, I was not even able to walk for exercise, and I gained over fifty pounds. Because I submitted to a life style of change, all of this frustration did not divide our family. I made small changes at first. About four years ago, I asked the Lord to help me lose weight and to heal the eating disorder. As He began work on this emotional aspect of the injury, I had to choose to walk every day. My doctor released me to do this and I began with fifty feet, then a hundred feet at a time. It took me several years to build up to a half mile and now I walk about twenty minutes a day, five days a week. My blood pressure began to decrease along with my stress level, improving my sense of well-being while I lost forty pounds. It didn't come overnight, but I didn't allow my feelings to rule my daily activities. I learned patience and a new kind of discipline. I forced myself to change my eating habits and learned to walk for exercise under my doctor's supervision. In this way, I produced a more relaxed atmosphere for myself and the entire family, and better communication for all of us. So be encouraged. Whatever mountain you have to climb, it can be done!

Changing Unacceptable Behavior

Unacceptable behavior can be changed through proper communication. We can choose to treat one another the way we want to be treated. As I said earlier, my wife was the individual who showed me Christ-like love. Her compassion, her touch, her notes of encouragement, many times, gave me the spark in hopeless situations to hang onto God's love and His Word. By her approaching me in love, I was able to deal with unacceptable behavior, like violent temperament. At times, we need to approach our spouses or our children, whether they live with us or not, regarding behavior that is unacceptable. It is our responsibility to approach them in love with the encouragement they need to make changes. No woman, as an example, should have to live in an atmosphere of fear. She might have to speak to her husband with a counselor, compassionately and firmly, but it must be made known that the behavior is unacceptable and will not be tolerated.

Again, this is a day of new beginnings. Make small changes in your life. As you do this, the Lord will give the whole family the desire and attitude necessary to challenge for change!

Remember:
1. The Golden Rule
2. Learn positive new problem-solving approaches.
3. Determine to come into agreement with your spouse.
4. Pray, pray, pray.
5. Affirm each other often.

CHAPTER SIX

"FORGIVE US... AS WE FORGIVE..."

It is the will of God for us to walk in forgiveness. The Bible teaching on this is very clear. Jesus Himself taught us to pray, "forgive us our debts as we forgive our debtors" (Matthew 6:12). The dynamic force of forgiveness comes when we receive Jesus Christ into our hearts and lives, into every aspect of our being. It starts with a decision to ask Him for forgiveness of our own sins and a new start. You may have been deeply wounded, even abused, and struggle with forgiving others. However, we all have come short of the mark God has set for us and need to begin with His forgiveness. This begins the only process by which we can truly forgive those who have hurt us. Jesus goes on to say in verses 14 and 15, "For if you forgive men their trespasses, your heavenly Father will also forgive you: but if you forgive not men their trespasses, neither will your Father forgive your trespasses." The mandate is clear. Then we will be able to start receiving peace, understanding and God's wisdom for life.

Even when we have forgiven others who have hurt us, many of us have a difficult time forgiving ourselves. I know this from my own personal experience. We feel we are unworthy or undeserving of God's love and forgiveness. Well, the truth is we are all undeserving. God doesn't love us because we are good. He loves and forgives us because HE IS GOOD. No matter how good or bad our lives are, no matter what we have or have not done, none of us deserves God's favor. But He extends it anyway because of Who He is. The cross levels the playing field. When you rest with that, you can approach God to receive forgiveness, cleansing and a new start, and just be thankful. Remember, those who are forgiven much, love much (Read Luke 7:36-50).

Let me take you on a short journey through the process of forgiveness which will cause God's blessing to flow toward you. Keep in mind that God loves all people, but He has a covenant with you, a special commitment to those who have chosen to receive His love and forgiveness through His Son. He has promised to heal and restore.

Forgiveness starts with a choice of your free will. This choice should not be determined by feelings, no matter how hurt you are, how much rejection you feel, or how much suffering you've been through. The choice to forgive is just that, a choice. Once you make it, God can equip you to begin a life style of forgiving. Start with yourself. You will find that forgiveness is the door to transformation, so begin the renewing process. Confess your feelings of failure, rejection, or helplessness right now. Choose to speak words of forgiveness over the people who have hurt you. You might want to name them right now. You can say, "Even though my feelings have not changed, by the power I receive from the Lord, I forgive so-and-so". When the feelings crop up from time to time, restate your decision – "I forgive so-and-so in the name of the Lord", and do not entertain thoughts or feelings of hostility against them. Affirm your decision as often as you need to. Words are powerful! In time, you will walk free of the resentment and bitterness of past events. The feelings will fade and forgiveness will become a very real part of your being. Sometimes I had to write letters to the Lord explaining situations and offering forgiveness to others. The letters were never sent. They were just tools to help me put down the hurt and rejection of my past and allow the Lord to cleanse me so I could walk in forgiveness. This doesn't leave much room for self-pity. I could then expect Him to work on my behalf because I had taken to heart His commands to forgive and to love others as ourselves.

Once you receive God's forgiveness and accept your past as forgiven, you can accept the idea that the future can be completely different. You are not a second-class family living under a cloud, but you can live under the blessing and provision of God through His mighty Word.

The first step then, is the CONSCIOUS CHOICE TO FORGIVE, even though your hurt feelings might be very much alive. The mere fact that you and I do not hate some people is a miracle. The ability to wish them well and pray God's blessing upon them is evidence of forgiveness. By praying for those who have hurt you and lied against you, God is free to work on your behalf and theirs. He can begin to draw them to Himself toward the greatest blessing of all, true relationship with Himself.

Having handled many domestic disputes, I came to the realization that there needs to be forgiveness and cleansing on both sides. All parties are hurting, and even after remarriage, the need to forgive and receive forgiveness often remains. Dealing with a former spouse will be a part of life until your children are grown. Beginning with the basic building blocks of forgiveness, you can make life more peaceful, healing and pleasant for all involved. If the other party does not receive this, that is not your choice. You are being obedient to the Lord's command. Ask forgiveness for anything you have done which caused hurt, and request that you work with each other over the years for the best interest of your children. This may take time to develop, but it's worth the effort.

Legal Implications

Like myself, many of you were divorced before coming into relationship with the Lord. Unfortunately, there are many Christians who were, or are, in circumstances of violence, abandonment or other forms of gross mistreatment. We do not have to feel guilty or condemned. We all can be renewed through the grace of the Lord and given a new beginning. As mentioned earlier, some children live in abusive situations involving a parent or the live-in friend of a parent. In cases like these, one needs to pray about possible pursuance of custody before a tragedy occurs. The first course of action is to speak to the parent in this life style and try to help him or her give the child a healthy environment. If after a reasonable time, this does not have any effect, one should pray and seek counsel, and if the situation warrants, contact an attorney and begin a court proceeding. Mothers should usually raise the children, but as stated before, there are exceptions.

A decision like this to gain custody of one's children will be costly, not only financially, but also emotionally and psychologically for all parties involved. The court system is there as a safety net for your children. Once you contact an attorney and paperwork is begun, the court generally will send all parties for evaluation to child and family counseling with a psychiatrist or psychologist, and this can be a lengthy procedure. Emotions can run very high on all sides. You will need to remain calm and focused, and allow the Lord to be your shield and defense. Be prepared for possible false accusations while going through this process, but remember that truth will outlive a lie. Once the counseling and evaluation are completed, a report will be made to the court and there is always the possibility of a trial. A ruling will be made by the judge and, prayerfully and hopefully, the child's best interest will be served. Remember, God wants all children raised in a peaceful home, free from abuse of any kind. If there are parents who take this course of action, they must do so without bitterness, but with genuine concern for the welfare of their children. Men who make this decision must still treat the mothers of their children with respect and dignity, trying to help them in any way possible, even after the rendering of a court decision. Forgiveness is all important.

The same is true for ladies reading this. Perhaps you are in a situation where the support for your child is not coming in or is very irregular. You see your children lack and often times, you go without. Often the child support is affordable, but the other parent's life style does not line up with the responsibility. Walk in forgiveness even though it hurts. If there is no productive communication, you also have the option of using the legal system. Again, this will be costly financially and emotionally. This process can take time to resolve issues. It's difficult and full of delays, but as long as we walk in forgiveness with the best interest of our children at heart, the Lord will make a way. There may be times when you will have an appointment with the court and your case will be postponed. You may be frustrated, hurt and angry, but you must release your feelings to the Lord. He knows what is best. Judges often rotate and serve specific periods of time on the bench. We know of situations where various attorneys and judges were moved off the court docket by the timing of the court system. We found that judges who then heard these particular cases were better suited to make favorable judgments by their very expertise.

Don't concentrate on the "whys". Trust that as you put your faith in God, He will take control of your situation. DON'T SPEAK NEGATIVELY about the parties involved to your children or to anyone else. PRAY for the person you are taking to court for his or her salvation, well-being, provision and, of course, for a change of heart where the children are concerned. Also, TRY TO SETTLE OUT OF COURT on some points. There might be more common ground than you think. This is difficult but very practical. Keeping a right attitude of heart will bring the power of God to bear on your situation. KEEP CONFRONTATION TO A MINIMUM and RELEASE YOUR EMOTIONS through prayer so that you can walk in peace as much as possible. Again, by operating in the principle of forgiveness and perseverance, trusting the Lord to work through the system, you can have a long-term positive effect on the children whose well-being is at stake.

"They Know Not What They Do"

An example of forgiveness in our family occurred several weeks after Lee and I were married. One of our sons decided he did not want to live at home and packed his bags to go live with his father. If I would have allowed this, I would have been shirking my responsibility and obligation to my new family to which I committed myself before the Lord. You might ask, "Why would he do this?" Keep in mind the rejection, hurt and guilt children go through without the ability to process these feelings and experiences. Out of his hurt and confusion, he left and I took the position of calling his father. We discussed this and I gave him a few days to stay there and think things over before he was expected home. If I had allowed him to stay indefinitely, he would have established a life pattern of running from pressure, obligations and his own feelings. By not allowing him to stay away, I was able to help him start working on forgiveness from his point of view toward those who had hurt him.

In a new marriage, remember the power of agreement when dealing with an ex-spouse. For ladies who are dealing with males who still treat you with disrespect and intimidation, there needs to be positive action from you and your husband. Don't allow the spirit of fear to rule, but know that it's natural for your feelings to go up and down. Having forgiven and determined to walk in an attitude of love, truth and peace, you can regain your dignity and the necessary support to help raise your children. Again, work this out amicably, if possible. If not, there is the legal system. As you work through the system, don't stop giving, even though finances may be tight, because the

Lord will bless the seed you sow for abundant provision later on.

Choice Equals Change

The scriptures are full of examples of people who chose to forgive rather than to hold loved ones or others who hurt them in the bondage of bitterness or resentment. This action and attitude to forgive "uncuffs" the Lord's hands allowing Him to work on our behalf. If we hold hatred or bitterness in our hearts, God can not work in our situations. Remember, this is not a feeling but a choice we can make, expecting God to respond according to His Word. In the book of Genesis, chapters 39-50, we see the prime example of Joseph, a young man who was sold into slavery by his brothers who hated and rejected him because of jealousy. No matter where he went, even as a slave, he had the favor of God on his life. Why? - because He chose to forgive and to serve those around him, refusing to rehearse the past. He chose to serve even his captors with a forgiving attitude. As we know, he became the chief servant of Potiphar's house where he would be falsely accused by his master's wife who tried to seduce him many times. Yet, he said he could not commit such a sin in the sight of God and his master. Joseph had determined to love as God loves. He did not have scriptures or tapes to study from, or regular teaching and preaching. HE LIVED OUT OF THE LOVE OF GOD IN HIS HEART. We know the story, He became second in command in Egypt and his family eventually settled there and was spared during a great famine. God allowed these trials, tribulations and sufferings in Joseph's life so he could be a blessing to the nations and to those who had hurt him.

You and I, too, can be a blessing to those who have hurt us deeply. By choosing to forgive, we give God the freedom to change us and our circumstances. As we let this work out to those around us, we can focus on God's will and purpose for our lives and our families. As we walk in forgiveness, we do not allow our past to dictate our future. Our minds will replay or revisit the hurts and sufferings again and again. We will not forget them, but we will forget the pain attached to them. God will heal us and we will be able to discuss what we have been through, at times, to minister help to others. He will bring beauty instead of ashes and enable us to bless others out of our experience.

When you fail and ask your family for forgiveness, you set the tone for them by demonstrating the principle. We all learn best by example, and this is a good seed to plant in your family to help bring them out of the "victim" mentality. They will learn that they do not have to feel hurt and devastated for the rest of their lives. There is a higher road. In Genesis 50:19 and 20, we read that Joseph said, "You meant this for evil against me, but God meant it for good in order to save many people". Choose this Godly attitude demonstrated at the cross when our Savior cried out, "Father, forgive them for they know not what they do" (Luke 23:34). Many times, a former spouse, a parent, a school teacher or even someone in ministry may have hurt us or lied about us. As we say this to our heavenly Father – "forgive them for they know not what they do" – He will cleanly erase the pain from our own hearts. He will restore us, permitting us to go about our business as He intended, leaving the brokenness behind. We can then help put the pieces back together in other people's lives, too. When you choose to forgive, God helps you go on to a greater calling.

Joseph also had hope in the midst of what appeared to the natural eye to be a hopeless situation. This wasn't the hope the world offers, that perhaps something good will happen. This was REAL HOPE in a REAL GOD who sends REAL POWER to effect REAL CHANGE. Even when circumstances don't change right away, God will change you, if you permit Him, so that you are not devastated in the midst of your situation. You can become strong enough to outlast and overcome any adversity as you release your "right" to be angry and bitter. It is difficult to explain the power and freedom that flows from forgiveness. You must experience it as Joseph did.

Conclusion

As we put our faith, hope and love together, our family and our future will be on solid ground. It's interesting to note that Joseph had two children while he was in Egypt. He named the first son Manasseh which means "made to forget all sorrow and past". Here he was, second in command of the strongest nation in the world, and he chose to honor the living God by giving his children Hebrew names in the court of Pharoah. Yes, Joseph declared that God blessed him and made him forget his past sorrow. He named his second son Ephraim which means "God made me fruitful in the land of pain". God will also make YOU fruitful through your pain and suffering, and even in the midst of it. He will equip you to help individuals around you, even those who have hurt you, and to change circumstances like your former ones for many others. You can overcome obstacles the way we did, and continue to do, in our family. We did not allow circumstances to dictate to us, but rather talked and prayed and lived out the love and forgiveness that we have been given by the Lord. This is a new day, a new beginning. Rest in God's love, speak His Word out loud right now, thank and praise Him, and hold onto that hope, as Joseph did, that the Word of God will be the driving force in your life and your family. Don't go by what you see around you, but live by the promises of the living God. Forgiving others as God has forgiven you will erase pain and sorrow so that you can walk with your head high and your heart free.

Remember:
1. Forgiveness is a choice.
2. Feelings will line up with your choices in time.
3. Dangerous situations may require legal help.
4. Forgiveness uncuffs God's hands to work for you.
5. Choice equals change.

CHAPTER SEVEN

MONEY MATTERS

It is the will of God for your family to be stable and to prosper so that you can sow into the lives of others. The area of finances in the blended family is complex and thus, produces a great possibility for stress and division between husband and wife. There are several reasons for this added pressure. First, there are often financial obligations to children of a previous marriage, so money is leaving the household every month to help support them. Second, child support that may be coming into the home is often not sufficient to keep up with the rising cost of living and, in some instances, is paid sporadically or not at all during the period of obligation. The couple must handle this situation, together with other financial decisions, with truth, compassion and wisdom from God. Keep in mind that the Lord wants your marriage to succeed and He wants not only to meet your needs, but also to give your new family financial stability as well. As you work out your budgeting, which I will talk more about later, remember that His will for you is TO BE STABLE and TO PROSPER.

The majority of men would rather not discuss and change how they handle the money they make because they regard the subject as very personal. Because they earn money, they feel it is theirs and can be spent as they wish. However, in submission to the Lord there needs to be a new sense about Who gave you the ability to work and earn a living. Even though you may have sacrificed to go to school and prepare for your work, it is still the Lord Who gives you the ability and strength to work, Who keeps you safe at the workplace, and Who will increase your business if you are self-employed (Deuteronomy 8:18). Regardless of what work you perform – professional, construction, management or labor – all resources are the Lord's and He's given you the ability to become financially stable. Men, if you want to see your wife and children come alongside you and support you, show them that you are willing to learn and to make changes when it comes to your finances. As you make changes, remember that God loves you and has your best and that of your family in mind. He wants you to succeed. He does not want failure to dominate your life. He has given you the blueprint and the tools to accomplish your goals. Change takes time.

As we have read, our worth and value are in the person of the Lord Jesus Christ and we find His ways through His Word. It is through developing this relationship with Him that we find our true worth. It is not how much money we make, what kind of clothes we wear, what type of vehicle we drive, not even the degrees we have, the size of our ministry, or who accepts us that is important. It's what God says about us that is important and our willingness to live according to His Word. Our obedience will cause us to prosper physically, mentally, spiritually, financially and in every way so that we may do God's work in the world.

Let's talk about an important principle which is all but forgotten in America. That is that financial success is LIVING WITHIN YOUR INCOME. Doing this over a long period of time will produce financial stability. Many times we say, "If I only made more money..." when the truth is we often need to manage better what we have. Look at the entertainment and sports industries where individuals make a great deal of money. Most of them live by "the more you make, the more you spend" principle. I'm sure you have read about people who have gone bankrupt making multiple millions of dollars. The same rules apply to us no matter what our income. If we don't learn to examine our motives, our true values and our spending habits, no amount of money will be enough to satisfy us. If we get a thousand dollar raise, we will want to spend two thousand. If we get a five thousand dollar raise, we will want to spend ten. If we get a dollar raise, we will want to spend as though we make two dollars more an hour. The principle is the same.

Invite your spouse and family in to help establish productive financial goals and patterns. Start where you are and continue to develop a spirit of thanksgiving for your talents and God-given ability to get wealth.

A Life Style of Giving

As we examine our ways, keep in mind that God is not held to our scope of wisdom on money management. Our way is to get and to hang onto. His way is to earn, to save and to give so that we can partner with Him, making sure the message and the love of God is provided to those around us. As we learn to put into use the various aspects of Biblical stewardship – CHEERFUL GIVING, WISE BUYING and SOUND BUDGETING – God can entrust us with more resources. He owns it all to begin with, and we are only caretakers or stewards for a short season. He wants to entrust us with more so that we can not only be blessed ourselves, but freely bless others. The difficulty is not in God giving us resources, abilities or talents, but with us releasing what He has already given us. God will multiply what you have when you are faithful in helping others. The world would say to horde when you have a need, but God says to give. A little with God's blessing on it will go farther than a lot with no blessing. Do you ever feel like you are putting your money in a bag with holes in it? You get a little saved and the car needs repair, the kids need clothes, the hot water tank breaks, or someone's teeth need straightening? This happens when you have no seed in the ground and no expectation of a harvest. When you give cheerfully, God blesses your harvest, not only to abundantly meet your needs but also the needs of others.

We have the example of the Roman centurion in the gospels who sent to the Lord to ask for the healing of his servant (Matthew 8). You know the story. Jesus wanted to go to his house but the centurion said, "Lord, I am not worthy that you should come under my roof, but just speak the word and my servant will be healed". Jesus here made mention of faith hand-in-hand with obedience to authority. This centurion understood obedience to authority. As a police officer, I also understood obedience to authority and I continued to learn the importance of making financial decisions in obedience to Biblical principles. Not only did I give faithfully to my local church, but I also gave regularly to other ministries and individuals to help meet their needs. In other words, by depositing our resources in good ground, we provide opportunity for God to entrust us with more.

Through The Valley

I began to give into the kingdom of God before I was married, while I was healthy and able to work extra jobs and had resources coming in on a regular basis. At Christmas, I would make sure the single mothers of our congregation had gifts, toys for their children and food. I worked with the local church on this, but most of these items were made possible through the extra security jobs I worked during the holiday seasons. After my injury in 1981, I could not work at all resulting in a season of my life with no income at all. I was now married with the responsibility of a wife and four children. Eventually, after receiving my "performance of duty disability", I began to receive half-pay based on the year it was granted. This was a fixed income and would not increase. Most people would question why this happened to me. I never concentrated on the "whys". Many thought I should stop giving at this time. However, I continued to give cheerfully and developed a pattern of "living and giving".

As I said, I was unable to go out of my home a great deal or to any kind of work, so I would try to do some housework while my wife was at work and the kids were at school. If someone at church was recovering from an illness or had a family crisis, I cooked a meal and made sure it was brought to them. This enabled me to start getting my eyes off my own problems. My wife and I, in conjunction with a ministry we served, would write local toy manufacturers at Christmas time, and they would donate enough toys for sixty to seventy children. Together with our children, we would wrap the gifts, load our pick-up truck and go to the inner city. We left the gifts with a local pastor to be distributed to needy families, especially single-parent families. I've always had a burden for children and struggling moms, and holidays are particularly strained for them. These gifts, toys, blankets and food continued to move out of our home even though my income was very limited. This taught our children to GIVE OUT OF A NEED and to DEVELOP A SPIRIT OF PRAISE AND THANKS. As you meet the needs of others, you enable the Lord to meet your needs abundantly. We never kept any of these gifts for our own children, but each holiday the Lord would provide an abundance of love, peace and gifts for the family to share. This was also an opportunity for the children to see the needs of others, helping to mold them into compassionate adults. Today they continue in this life style – giving of their time, their talents and their resources to meet the needs of people who come across their paths. Whether it's fixing someone's car, baby-sitting, bringing groceries or lending a helping hand in some other way, this life style is now second-nature to them. It also brought many blessings to those helped because it showed that God's love has no boundaries or barriers except what we place on it. If we are obedient in putting the needs of others first, especially as heads of the home, we can create this life style in our families.

For many years, I sacrificed clothing and other necessities for myself so that my wife and children would have necessary provisions, paid bills, and the opportunities for sports, dance lessons or other activities that would help them meet their goals as they were growing. When our oldest son graduated from Christian school, he wanted to attend Bible college out of state. I chose to sell some of my possessions such as hand guns, equipment and tools, a camera, a truck and plow, and eventually, a piece of land on which I previously planned to build a log cabin. Over the fourteen years, I sold belongings because they had no meaning to me in light of the needs of my family. Out of obedience to the Lord, I sold these things at a fair price so as to bless the buyers and help meet the cost of our son's college education. I didn't do it grudgingly, but cheerfully, knowing God's Word is true. If we remain faithful in the valley and not let the circumstances dictate to us, we can choose in faith to rise above the situation that was dealt to us. When we operate this way, there is surely no weapon formed against us that will be able to prosper. Family members that love one another and work together will rise above any adversity, although the choice may go against our feelings at first. FEELINGS SHOULD NOT DICTATE OUR ACTIONS. As we choose for the higher good, the very things that might have destroyed us will actually help us grow and overcome adversity.

Changing Your Financial Future

Remember, all resources are the Lord's and He has given you the ability to become a steward or caretaker of what He entrusts to you. DO NOT ATTACK EACH OTHER or blame one another for your financial situation. Choose rather to walk in forgiveness, to walk as a team, and to search the scriptures together on all aspects of finance. Start by THANKING and PRAISING THE LORD already for taking you out of debt, putting you on solid ground and preventing you from becoming like the majority of people who let circumstances dictate their financial future. There are many voices attempting to influence you in the area of finances, from Wall Street to co-workers. If you are in the ministry, don't look to people to supply your needs. God is our Source, but we must choose to believe this and act upon it. Every couple has the ability to change the direction of its family. It might take several years to achieve the goal of getting out of debt, depending on your situation, but you can accomplish it through a life style of giving.

Where Do You Want To Go?

Prayerful financial planning is LIFE PLANNING. There are two types of people in the world. The first type deliberately sets goals for themselves and their families. These people learn how to budget and will make the necessary adjustments and discipline themselves to stay with the aches and pains for a season to establish financial stability for the long term.

The second type of person does not plan, but only reacts and responds to life situations. These are usually undisciplined individuals who do not take responsibility well and choose not to deal with issues. If you ask them how they are, if they would be honest, they would say they are miserable. This is a result of choosing not to change and simply reacting in their feelings. They take this attitude into buying. They become frustrated or angry and go out to buy clothing or other articles that make them feel better for the moment. This does not help them overcome their failure to deal with life, and they become compulsive buyers enslaved to easy credit. This type of person does not want to be accountable to anyone – to God, to a spouse, to parents, to a boss, or to any authority figure. He or she does not even want to be accountable to him or herself to make changes.

Before we can change our situations, we need to examine ourselves. Instead of looking at the faults of everyone else, we need to look in the mirror and ask God for wisdom and strength to change ourselves. An important step in the process of change is goal-setting. What do you want to accomplish a month from now, six months from now, a year from now? It is known that the most disciplined and successful people are those who write their goals on paper and take specific steps to reach them. The main reasons people do not set goals are fear of failure, fear of change, lack of discipline or know-how and, oddly enough, fear of success. What will be expected of me if I accomplish my goals? Evaluate yourself in this area, and then write down some things you would like to accomplish on a short-term basis and then on a long-term basis. List some specific steps you can take to reach those goals. You can change if you determine to do so with God's help. Be faithful and persistent in seeking the Lord and in the things you have listed to help you reach your goals. Remember, God's will is for you to be financially stable and able to bless others, and He will grant you the wisdom to achieve it. It takes hard work and dedication to fulfill purpose, and it's worth it! You and I can not change the past, and we can not worry about the future, but if we choose to follow God's blueprint, we can make changes today that will affect our future and our destiny. Think of it. The choice is yours.

Your True Source

I learned that the police department was not my provision. THE LORD IS MY SOURCE, my strength, my shield and my provision and He is yours also. The more we operate in that understanding, the more we will see His promises fulfilled. Because budgeting in the blended family can be complex, we must work it out very wisely. As mentioned before, there is often child support either coming into the home or exiting the home. If you go to a bank for a remodeling loan, for example, many banking institutions count incoming child support as part of your income. Even though they choose to do this, I caution against it. We have ministered to couples who have done this and felt the adverse effect of making choices dependent on someone else's faithfulness to pay support. Quite simply, it is not wise to count on this money to help buy a bigger house or to remodel, even though the bank permits it. It is not uncommon for persons to default on support payments through loss of job or injury, or simply deciding not to pay. By not counting on this money, you guard your family against this outside influence dictating your future. If you have need of a bigger house, put the principles of Biblical finance into use. Start by GIVING and SAVING and the Lord will provide ways of accomplishing your goals without depending on outside finances. If this money comes in every month like it should, that's a plus. You can then use it in other ways and keep a hedge around our family from outside trouble at the same time. In preparation for budgeting, remember that you can help put the pieces back together in everyone's life through stability in this area.

We all know of situations where financial obligations to children are not met. How do you handle it when the money stops coming in? First of all, DO NOT BLAME ANYONE, whether they have a legitimate reason or not. Do not let their actions dictate your financial soundness. As I stated, do not count on this income for major expenditures in the home or for the upgrading of an automobile, for example.

Let me share the experience of one family as to how they handled the loss of child support. First, they did not become bitter or upset, but sat down and discussed their options. The father had been a partner in a small firewood business and found that he was able to buy out his partner's half of the business by making payments from selling cords of wood. Together with his children, he ran this business for almost three years. They had logs trucked in, then cut, split and stacked the wood, and delivered it with their truck. The business was very successful during this time of need. The money that stopped coming in had been used for food and other necessities, so the wood business met those needs. The children did a good job and learned much about hard work and giving through the experience. In the midst of their need, they would find people who needed firewood and give it to them at no cost. Of course, God ran to meet their needs because of their giving spirit. They all stayed healthy and strong, too, as they reached out to others with their goods and services.

Give of your time and talents. You might be able to fix an automobile, or do yard work or help someone with budgeting or child care. Partner with God in the business of giving and blessing others.

These children saw and experienced the blessing of God in their work as He kept them safe and provided for them in many ways. There was very little breakdown of their equipment and they had no major injuries. They learned much from their father's example. About three years later, the financial obligation was resumed and they were able to get out of the business, but this was a season of working and growing together for the entire family. During that time, the Lord provided a used snowmobile for the children which gave them lots of fun after their long hours of hard work. It was obvious that God's blessing extended beyond meeting their needs to giving them pleasure and enjoyment.

One of the concepts this family learned was team work. Someone has aptly said that the word team means "Together Effectively Achieving a Mission". As you create a team attitude in your family, you can effectively achieve your mission which, in this case, is financial soundness. You will also discover blessing upon other areas of your life in matters beyond money. In this case, the lack of outside resources could have caused division in the family, but it strengthened them instead. In the end, it's not so important what happens to you in life, but how you handle it that counts. Developing a Christ-like attitude makes the difference and will turn a situation that was meant for harm into good.

Remember:
1. It is God Who gives you the ability to get wealth.
2. Live within your income.
3. Evaluate your spending habits.
4. Learn to "sow seed".
5. Be a T.E.A.M.

CHAPTER EIGHT

BUDGET OR BUST!

It is God's will for you to operate in principles that will stabilize even the next generation. As you handle your present income according to God's proven methods, you become a better steward of your resources and you deposit into His financial system of accounting. No matter what occurs around you, you will not be shaken. Your attitudes about money will change into more Godly ones such as cheerful and faithful giving, helping others and giving out of a need. As you continue to do these things, you can expect the Lord to move on your behalf according to His Word.

There are several budget worksheets in the Appendix. You may want to experiment with them, modify them, or draw up your own suited to your family's needs. One way to begin is to get small notebooks and for the first thirty days, husband and wife should keep track of every purchase made down to a cup of coffee or a newspaper. Every item you buy should be recorded with its cost. At the end of the thirty days, you will have a gauge of how you spend money. As I said earlier, many of us say we need more money, when in reality, we need to become better managers of what we have. We can learn to live at a higher level of economy on the same amount of money as we gain a new perspective on resources.

I gave this advice to all our children and each found some money wasted on every day expenses. For example, it cost much less for one of them to bring coffee to work and for another to carry a lunch rather than purchase one. You might think these are small expenses, but add them up after thirty days. You will see that you can spend thirty or forty dollars a month for coffee, pop, candy or other small items you don't really need. This thirty day test is usually very productive. You will see some areas where you can make changes. You might decide to bring your lunch occasionally, or to skip lunch once a week and take a walk instead. You may decide to carpool, to share newspapers or to switch those expensive, sugary snacks for fruit or salad which will benefit you in other ways too.

Now that you have made some changes based on the thirty day test, establish a budget including tithing and giving, rent or mortgage, food, clothing, insurance, vacation, etc. For several years, you might not be able to take your family away a great deal for vacations, but that's okay. There are probably many recreational places near where you live that could be enjoyed by the whole family inexpensively. Find parks, beaches, museums, activity centers, and other places of interest. Picnicing, church socials and other group activities are usually inexpensive, allowing you to save for debt reduction. Camping and boat outings can be fit into even a modest budget. You don't have to spend thousands of dollars on vacations and put yourself in credit bondage to get away and enjoy some recreation. There will be a time down the road when, if you choose to take an extended vacation, you will be able to do so without credit card debt and with the cash saved to enjoy it.

Remember, your long-term goal of getting out of credit card debt as you sit together each month to write out checks for your tithe and your bills. Re-examine, refigure and fine tune your budget. Make this opportunity a teaching one for the entire family. Show your children by your checkbook, from an early age, that by tithing and giving regularly, you produce long-term financial stability. Explain the reasons why the whole family is making adjustments. This is an excellent opportunity to begin showing them how to set short and long term goals for themselves, and how to weigh the pluses and minuses of each purchase. By bringing the children into this, you are reinforcing the prioritizing of needs, wants and desires. Getting out of debt will not only free up resources and take pressure off the family, but also train your children to do the same.

Approach this with a good working attitude, realizing it's a wise investment of time to help you meet those important long-range goals. You may want to provide for summer camps or private schools, for example. Look at money management with a spirit of thanksgiving and expectancy, looking for blessing on your finances as you operate more by the rules of God's economy. As you make financial decisions, remember not to attack each other but attack the problem at hand. You will gain a real strength and joy knowing you are blessing your children and others as you give. As you partner with ministries that help children, for example, you can have an impact on lives around the world. You may want to help people in inner cities or on reservations or any number of other charitable works worthy of your support. These acts of charity are immeasurable, not only in themselves, but also in terms of what they teach your children and the variety of ways they come back to you in blessing. You safeguard your home and family, according to God's Word, when you meet the needs of others. Put the principles of good stewardship into use and work at your budget for six months to a year, tailoring it to your specific needs. Give regularly and cheerfully, knowing that you are sending the message of God's love to others who have little or no hope without your help.

In developing your budget, be willing to work together and to listen to each other's ideas. Honestly evaluate your present spending habits and set some attainable goals like paying off credit cards, having a savings account, a Christmas club, a needed vehicle, and so on. As you fine tune, here are some tips on making the most of the money you now have.   Some may be new to you, others may not.

The first area is grocery shopping. DO NOT SHOP WHEN YOU ARE HUNGRY. You will invariably buy more products that look appetizing to you at the moment. Supermarket competition is so keen today that each store has its own brand which is comparable to the nationally advertised brands at a much lower cost. Grocers usually put the most expensive products at eye level, so look above and below these expensive items for similar STORE BRANDS and you will spare your budget. Another strategy is checking the END-OF-AISLE displays for sale items and discontinued products which are very good. Obviously, COUPON CLIPPING is very popular with some shoppers. It takes time but it's worth the effort. Do it jointly or with the children and again, teach them to make the most of their resources.

Second, you can also cut your UTILITY BILLS. Have your home checked for INSULATION. Many utilities offer this service free and give you a checklist on how to improve your insulation value. Insulation is generally inexpensive and some utility companies offer special loans to those who qualify to help increase the R-value of your home. Insulating one room per year such as an attic, then a bedroom, etc. is one way of achieving your goal without borrowing money. After you take care of the insulation, CHECK YOUR DOORS AND WINDOWS. By replacing one or two per year, you can have all new doors and windows by the end of four or five years. This will not only save money on energy bills, but will also make your property look better and make the house quieter and warmer as well. There might be people at your church who can help you do some of these projects if you don't have the ability to do them yourself. Another utility to look at is the telephone. There are now companies with lower rates that donate a percentage of their proceeds to charitable organizations.

Other ways of saving money include checking into insurance companies for the best rates. Also, aside from items you want to give away, you might want to have a garage sale of good usable items. Not only have one but shop at garage sales for tools and other such reusable items at great savings. Most people can save money on clothing, too. Pray before shopping. Ladies can build a wardrobe with a few basic pieces enhanced by a variety of accessories – shoes, handbags, gloves, scarves and belts. These are fairly inexpensive items but they can be used with suits, jackets, skirts, dresses and slacks. Men who need to buy suits for business and other dress occasions should look in the paper. There hasn't been a time I needed a suit that I didn't pray and find the perfect suit at a sale price. I have shopped at the same store for years and receive sale fliers from them so I can take advantage of the best prices.

Reminder

The way to a successful family budget is TEAM WORK. Even though one might write the checks and pay the bills, both must know how much money is coming in and the expenses that are being paid so that there will not be disagreements as to how income is allotted. The spirit of unity is all important in how you handle your finances. Encourage one another in this area so that you tap into each other's insight. Whoever is better able to do the actual accounting should do it, but the decision making process needs to be a team effort if you are going to be successful.

Tools and Systems

There are many systems of budgeting. Initially, I used the simple envelope system for bill-paying – just a pad, paper and envelopes. Others may have computer systems.

However, don't go out and buy a computer and software for budgeting. Start with a simple plan of action. First, figure out your yearly expenses like insurance. Divide by twelve and put that amount in an envelope marked insurance each month. Figure your average utility bills and do the same. Everything that is due monthly, like rent and mortgage, should also have an envelope. Designate so much per week for food and each expense. Also have an envelope marked savings and try to put something in it every month. You may occasionally have to use it for an unexpected expense at first, but at least you won't have to charge it and pay interest. The idea is to get something started and build on it. By remaining faithful to this system, you will learn to live within your income and accomplish your goal of getting out of debt. What you put away in June for December's insurance payment needs to stay in the envelope, as well as June's contribution to the Christmas club. If you don't have it left over, don't spend it, and don't presume on the future by charging things you can not afford. Keep one envelope for each month and put all your receipts for the month into it. Mark each receipt with the check number and the date it was paid. Get a shoe box or a plastic box and keep all the envelopes in order. In other words, if there is any question about a bill being paid, you have an orderly system of receipts to demonstrate what is paid and what is owed. This is a definite plan of action. It works and it's something anyone can do. If you have software for budgeting, use it, or you may have another simple system that works. It is not necessary to spend a lot of money in order to budget well. Use what you have. (See Appendix)

Debt Cancellation

In addition to the usual expenses and some credit card debt, my wife and I had a student loan. Being on half-pay,

I found myself having to contact the banking institution that held the loan. I explained about my injury and they said that if the loan were in my name, they could cancel the debt, but since it was in my wife's name, they could not. They did give me a six-month deferment during which I could make only the interest payment. This helped me to start paying off some of the other bills. At the end of the six month period as I continued to be faithful with the financial principles I am sharing, I contacted the bank again. My circumstances, to the natural eye, appeared to be getting worse in terms of my health and my income. However, I continued to believe that my healing was taking place and that my finances were already being increased. This is what I call having "believer's eyes". I contacted the bank explaining the situation for the second time and they said they would get back to me. Some months later, they called and stated that they decided to forgive the student loan even though that was not their usual policy! Yes, the Lord does cancel debts, and thus, I was able to concentrate on reducing our credit card debt.

This presuming on tomorrow is an attitude which has pervaded the church. It dictates to us that in order for us to be a success, to have worth, or to feel good about ourselves, we must have certain automobiles, certain clothing or other things. However, this is not true. If our whole life is taken up with acquiring things, in reality, those things own us. Remember, "the borrower is servant to the lender" (Proverbs 22:7). Acquiring a new inner attitude about money will free you from the willingness to put yourself in bondage to credit. Desire financial stability and freedom so you can be a blessing to the kingdom.

Remember:
1. Take the thirty-day test.
2. Set specific goals.
3. Be a giver.

4. Set up a budget that works for you.
5. Practice TEAM WORK.

CHAPTER NINE

TACKLING THAT MOUNTAIN OF DEBT

It is God's will for you to get out of debt and to get money working for you. There are several ways you can start the process. You can add up your credit card debt and find an existing card or a new one that has a lower interest rate for starters. Make sure you thoroughly research them, and then add all of your debt on the lowest interest-charging account, making sure you CANCEL THE OTHER CARDS after you pay them off with the single card. The important thing now is to keep your payment the same. In other words, if you were paying $200 per month to credit cards and now the minimum payment on your consolidation is $150, continue to pay the $200 per month. Thus, you will be able to pay down this loan at a faster rate.

Another plan is to take your credit cards that total, say $200 per month, and pay off the one with the smallest balance first. Now you might say, "I have an extra $50 per month to spend on something else". Don't do that. Continue to budget that same $50 per month together with your regular payment of, say $50, on another card and target that one for extinction. Now you will be paying $100 per month on the second card. Once you pay this one off, apply the same principle to the next and so on, using all the budgeted money, the whole $200 a month, toward the final credit card.

In addition to consolidation and paying down credit cards with the same amount each month until they are paid off, you can reduce your debt by SELLING ITEMS you and your family do not really need. Make a list of items you own, remembering your goal of getting out of debt, and the Lord will give you the desire of your heart. It will be accomplished with His principles operating from within. In

America, we have many storage facilities for items that we don't have enough room for in our homes or apartments.

The cities and countrysides are full of these storage sheds and many of the items in them are not even paid for! This is another example of the presumptuous mindset we have adopted. However, we are not going to operate in this attitude any longer, but rather in God's principles of financial freedom – independence from bondage and dependence upon Him. Sell unneeded items and put the money toward your credit debt. If you have exercise equipment you don't use or extra furniture, etc. sell it, pay off your bills and eventually, you probably won't even need the storage shed. Free yourself! Soon, instead of paying interest, you can start earning money through investments.

Another thing you will find as you accomplish your goals is that the Lord will give you overtime, sales will increase, or you will remain working while others may not. I know a construction worker who loved the Lord, but did not put these truths into use initially. As he grew in understanding and began to tithe and give, he no longer got laid off every year. In fact, in his line of work, which is seasonal in our part of the country, he continued to work when other members of his trade were not able to find work. This is one way the Lord showed him and his family favor and he was able to accomplish his goal of getting out of debt while others were not even paying the bills. As you do these things, expect God to increase your pay through overtime or extra sales, to protect your job, perhaps to give you something part-time for a season and also to make your money go farther and last longer. In obedience to God's ways, you will find greater freedom to enjoy the life that He wants you to have without financial worry (Malachi 3:8-11).

Mortgage Savings

Here are a few ways to save yourself thousands of dollars and years off your mortgage. First, take your regular monthly payment of, let's say $600, divide that in half and pay the bank a half payment every fourteen days. Many banks do offer a bi-weekly payment plan, so check yours. This alone will save you thousands of dollars in interest and take a significant number of years off your loan. Another way to accomplish mortgage payment reduction is by adding an extra $50 a month to your payment to be taken off the principle of your loan. Again, this will save you many years of payments and thousands of dollars in interest. You can give yourself and your spouse a present by making one additional payment a year on your mortgage, maybe from a tax return or money you don't have to pay on credit card debt any more. Just this one additional payment a year can save you thousands of dollars in interest. Search the scriptures and be convinced that God wants you free of debt. Then research the options offered to you through the banking institutions and you will find some ways and means to attain financial freedom and to give more to the work of the kingdom. Thus, you will be depositing in your heavenly account where there is never any recession, deflation or penalty, but only interest that accrues to you!

To Buy or Not To Buy!

Besides getting out of credit card debt and saving multiple thousands of dollars and years off your home mortgage, you can save on the cost of an automobile. If you already have a monthly auto payment, you should continue to pay that off and then continue to put that same amount of money in the bank where it can earn some interest for you. Instead of upgrading your car as soon as that note is paid, let that car serve you for many years. When it's time to buy another car, take the money you have saved and either pay cash for a slightly used car or put a great deal more money down on a new one making your monthly payments lower. You can follow this procedure over a period of years until you will be able to pay cash for your car. It seems rather difficult, but remember the principles stated here and always pray about your financial decisions.

Over the years when we had to upgrade our vehicles, I only had several thousand dollars to work with. Every time we would pray, the Lord would give us two choices. One would be a very fancy automobile and the other would be a sound, plain model. The choices were ours, but we always took the less extravagant model. In the long run, it proved out that as we made these choices with prayerful consideration, the Lord blessed and the vehicles lasted us for years. We were able to drive very safe vehicles that were well within our budget even though they were not brand new or fancy. We learned to avoid undue pressure by LIVING WITHIN OUR INCOME over a long period of time. This is an important key to establishing financial freedom.

Education

In a blended family, you might have older children when you marry and thus, not have the opportunity to save for years for their college education. However, there are ways to accomplish the goal of college education, trade school or vocational training they might choose. Let's talk about college first. The most obvious question is the type of school that the child wants to attend. This decision should not be left to the child alone as it involves many considerations such as programs, location, cost, etc. This should be decided through a process of research, discussion and prayer over a period of time. This process should not bring heartache but hope. As you point out to your children the pluses and minuses of various options, they are old enough to understand that they don't want to be saddled with a great deal of debt when they graduate from college. An ivy league school, as an example, costs five times as much as a state university. Initially, these ivy league schools were founded by Christians and built upon biblical principles, but many have strayed from those foundations. There are other private schools and state schools which offer good education, and can keep the cost within reach. Seventy-five per cent of all financial aid is awarded in the form of grants, loans and employment programs from the college and from our government. Even private Christian colleges are eligible for many of these grants and loans, and there are also work-study programs available.

Many scholarships go untapped every year simply because they are not researched by parents and students. The best way to find out about these scholarships is to research the college, the state education office, and even the high school guidance counselor's office. The counselor may not have much time to spend with you personally, but their books are available to you, and they will be glad to help you make contacts with those offering education money. There are also many businesses that offer grants and scholarships to students even without a relative in their business. These are worth seeking out. Make the process hopeful and cheerful, knowing that together, you are helping to build the future.

Some students do better staying at home and beginning at a two-year community college and then transferring to a four-year school. One of our sons did this and transferred all his credits to a state college to continue his education there. The community colleges also offer many technical courses and many of these schools have an eighty to ninety percent job placement rate after graduation.

Some children do well in the national armed services, too. Some people do not like this idea, but for some it is a way of accomplishing the child's goals. Many young people learn life-enhancing skills, teamwork and discipline in the service along with their particular college education and training. Some young people do not want to go to college but rather choose to pursue a technical skill. There are many programs available to help them reach their goals too. Career choices begin to form at an early age in most children. Our daughter, for example, has always wanted to be a paramedic and is now well on her way to fulfilling that goal. At first, I did not enthusiastically embrace the idea, but since I recognized that she is highly motivated in this area, I have done all I can to get her the best education to achieve her goal. Since the writing of this book began, she has been blessed with a wonderful scholarship and is working hard toward becoming a nurse/paramedic. I mentioned before selling items to pay for tuition and expenses, if necessary. The important factors are doing it together, looking at this as an opportunity to permit the Lord to show His faithfulness again, and encouraging your children that they are gifted and talented, and have purpose and destiny.

Many adults in the work place do not like what they do, but it does not have to be so for your children. Help them discover what is inside them. Let your children have opportunities to help and serve, and be exposed to a variety of individuals with unique callings and experiences. This will help them in the process of choosing a career. Giving a foundational college education to our daughters is important too, without losing sight of the fact that being a wife and mother is an important calling as well. We should train them at home for these responsibilities as well as providing for career goals. This is not necessarily an either/or situation, as many young wives and mothers also help earn income for their families. The same is true for our sons. No matter what they choose to do in life, it is our job to instruct them in how to become a Godly man and take care of every day responsibilities. This is not digressing from finances or college education, but incorporating the idea of LIFE TRAINING. We should not pressure our children, but bring them in on the financial decisions surrounding education so that we have a season of working with them on these choices.

A Fresh Start

Some who are reading this are anticipating marriage and a host of new household items to get them going. Many couples have said to us that buying everything new when they marry gives them a sense of a fresh start. They charge everything from pots and pans to furniture. Yes, they will have new surroundings but they will also have thousands of dollars worth of debt right from the start. This should be a big caution to all couples to start where you are. Whatever you had before you got married should be brought into your new family. Let the newness come from the love of God, your love for each other, and your determination to make a good home for each other and for your children. As you proceed together, you can add the things you desire to your home when you can pay cash for them and not put the family under undue pressure.

In our case, my wife had a small house when we got married and I was living in my mother's home. I moved into Lee's house and within four years, we were able to buy my mother's house where we raised our children until young adulthood. The Lord then provided us the opportunity and finances to buy our present home. Each of the other two houses was a blessing in its season. They served, not just our family, but others through Bible studies, food pantries and other ministry that flowed out of them. We established family traditions in those homes that carry over till today into the lives of our adult children. If you are able to have some new things right from the start without putting a financial burden on the family, by all means, have them. If, like most couples, you don't have extra money at the start, be thankful for what you have and be a good steward of what you are making. Soon you will be able to purchase the things you want without high interest payments as you establish a life style of giving to the Lord and having His blessing on what you keep. This is a new day, a new start.

Remember:
1. Pay your debts and get money working for you.
2. Research options.
3. Look for education money.
4. Live within your income.
5. Anyone can have a fresh start in God's economy by obeying His principles.

CHAPTER TEN

PARENTING IN THE BLENDED FAMILY

PART I

Obstacles Are Meant To Be Overcome

There are many voices in our society clamoring for our attention, wanting to tell us how to become effective parents. However, for the most part, we have lost sight of the only practical method of child-raising, and that is the time-proven principles in the Word of God. The Bible shows us that we are loved; it teaches us how we can forgive and be forgiven, and how we can grow and change. As our children watch us handle life according to the love of God and Biblical principles, they will develop a gauge for their decision-making process.

All parents, whether or not they have a blended family, go through seasons of frustration, anger, hurt or disappointment when children make choices contrary to their upbringing and contrary to the truths of God's Word. Some parents who have raised more than one child find that one of the children never allows him or herself to be healed or to deal with issues in his or her life. That child seems to be selfishly motivated and goes against all counsel, choosing to be unforgiving, for example, or a poor steward of resources. If you have a child like this, don't allow him or her, no matter what age, to place guilt and condemnation on you. Yes, you go through seasons of change yourself, but the same mercy and love of God which is there to help you change is available for them too if they are willing to pay the price. THERE IS A PRICE TO PAY TO BECOME A SOUND PERSON. Their behavior is not a reflection of you, but rather the result of wrong choices. If we are willing to begin where we are and make choices according to the truth, we can begin to overcome the obstacles in our pathway.

There are several main responsibilities of all Christian parents. The first is to take seriously a PERSONAL COMMITMENT to the Lord to live life on a daily basis so that our children can experience God's love through us, and our willingness to change. The second is that we MAKE OUR HOME A HAVEN for all family members where needs are met and all are included. This means creating an environment that produces growth, encouragement and a sense of self-worth and value. We all need a place to relax and just be ourselves. Thirdly, we must TEACH OUR CHILDREN to be responsible and faithful adults. They need to develop a good work ethic and find that there is satisfaction in the work of their hands. Fourth, it's important to ENJOY TIMES OF RECREATION together. Our children must learn that there is great joy in knowing God and that blessing follows our work and service. Laughter and enjoyment are necessary to good health and long life, and naturally reduce stress and anxiety. A "Sabbath" is not a good idea, it's a God idea. There are dozens of scripture verses that demonstrate these principles.

Stumbling Blocks or Stepping Stones?

Those of us who have chosen to be parents in a blended family will have unique challenges and obstacles to overcome in meeting our responsibilities. Remember it is the love, grace and mercy of God that will take any family that is scattered and hurt and weld it together into a family that is loving, caring, productive and on its way to fulfilling its destiny.

One of the fist hurdles encountered may be the influence of your child's other birth parent who might not be a believer or whose life style may be very different from your own. It takes diligence to counteract the effects of a negative environment in the other home where your child lives part of the time. The second presents itself when you marry with the expectation that the children you have chosen to raise will accept you, love you and appreciate you as if you were their birth parent. Depending on the age of the children, you should be aware that you could be in for a season of rejection and mistrust until the children are able to accept you in this new role and establish real, meaningful relationship. If you are aware of this possibility, you will not set yourself up for habitual hurt, rejection and division in the household. As you continue to love the children as Christ loves you, their love and appreciation for you will grow. It may take a long time or a little time. Every child is different. Continue to love them, teach them, correct them, guide and direct them. They will eventually be able to process their own hurt and rejection, and your love and acceptance will help them do that.

Children of divorce will usually look for any sign of affection from the birth parent with whom they do not live. Some children have a good relationship with this parent; some do not. If they do not, they will often have an unreal expectation and imagination of the relationship with that parent based on what they would like it to be. You must teach them not to set themselves up for continued hurt and rejection if this is the pattern that is occurring. The fact that they are valuable, lovable and special human beings must be reinforced to them often. As you help them through this stage, have patience with their feelings. Your guidance is extremely important. The more realistically they can view the relationship and accept it for what it is, the better they can deal with their emotions where that parent is concerned. As they become more secure in their relationship with you, they can learn to walk in forgiveness and to have open, trusting communication with you. These children will develop a sense of self-worth as you love them through their hurt and confusion into new and meaningful relationships. Remind them as often as necessary that you are not taking the place of their other parent, but that your relationship with them is unique and different. Again, each child is different and it takes some longer than others to cope with change and the healing process. AFFIRM THEM OFTEN.

Let's examine the example of a parent with visitation rights who calls and sets up a time to pick up the children, but then does not keep this date. There is no phone call or explanation. This behavior is repeated often as the children sit waiting, experiencing rejection time after time. What is your response to this? The first should be trying to discuss this action with the offending parent explaining that there needs to be a change for the benefit of the children. Encourage the parent to spend time with the children and keep his or her word regarding visits. If this parent takes your advice and whole-heartedly makes the change, it will mean a great step forward for the children. However, if this behavior persists, this is an opportunity to explain to the children that situations will exist in life in which people will not keep their word. This is not how you will treat people, but there are others who make promises they will not keep, and you will suffer disappointment. It's important that you allow them to tell you what they are feeling and experiencing. Let them empty out their hurt feelings and then pray with them, allowing the Lord to work in the situation. DON'T FEED THEIR ANGER and frustration with your own. BELIEVE IN GOD'S POWER to change people and old mind-sets. Over the months and years as you reinforce the love and value of your children, teaching them that they did not do anything wrong to cause themselves to be rejected, you will make a pathway for healing. DO NOT SPEAK NEGATIVELY about the other parent to or in front of the children. As they grow, they will develop a realistic gauge as to what the relationship really is. If you speak against that parent, you will not be operating in forgiveness and wisdom, and you will be feeding a negativism in them that will come back to you in many ways. Remember, all children will have disappointments. You have the opportunity to be a catalyst for healing, helping them through their hurts, and equipping them to have more positive relationships in the future. Pray with your children. Ask the Lord to touch their other parent with regard to the children's needs and their ability to be better able to handle this relationship. Resist bitterness, resentment and gossip. As you stay focused, you will help your family to do the same. You will watch your children go through different stages and adapt to the reality of old relationships and also new ones.

In our case, we made sure our children had birthday and Christmas gifts for their other parents, that they showed respect, and that they made phone calls when appropriate. Here are some examples of how our children handled these relationships.

One of our sons carried a lot of unforgiveness in his heart toward his father for leaving him at a young age, and possibly for other aspects of his life. When this child was about sixteen years old, he came to me and wanted to change his last name to mine. Some may think that was a good thing. However, I knew that in his heart, he wanted to do this to hurt his father. I chose to show him his need to forgive his father, and to relay some communication to him along those lines. I chose not to fuel the unforgiveness in him and he was able to overcome this.

When Lee and I married, one of our boys was ten years old. A few years later, he still had the unrealistic idea that he, his father and mother would someday be reunited and they would be a family again. Lee had been a single mother for some years when I met her, and the boys' father had already been remarried for several years. There was no cause for him to blame me for the divorce, but there existed in his mind this persistent, unhealthy idea that someday his birth parents would remarry. He showed some of his feelings toward me in the form of aloofness. We talked to him about this emotional holdover from his younger years and helped him deal with the reality of his parents' break-up, the value of allowing the Lord to heal him, the establishment of our new home, and the value of listening to our advice. When he graduated from high school at eighteen years of age, he chose to leave home and go on his own. I never chased him from the house, but I did pray that if any of the children chose not to be a part of the family, the Lord would move them for a season. This was the choice he made. However, within six months, he came home with a new attitude and a new heart, having written me a very touching letter expressing why he did some of the things he did as he was growing up, and I understood that.

Sometimes children will make you the scapegoat for their bitterness, animosity and even rejection, even though their hurt may have nothing to do with you personally. When you choose to help raise them, and they need and want that, they may still express anger over what they have been through previously. Understanding the root of their behavior will help you handle it without becoming offended all the time. I'm not talking about children showing disrespect, but hurt from continued disappointment and rejection. When you understand where they are coming from, you can focus more on their healing than on their anger.

Our daughter handled the situation much like one of the other boys did. We were granted custody of her when she was almost four years old, and when she would return from visits, she would sit with Lee and talk and cry, and cry and talk. This emptying out was her way of coping with her feelings from a very young age. Our other son was able to handle the adjustment to family life without much difficulty. He is very easy-going and forgiving by nature and accepts change more readily. Each one handles stress and pressure differently. Having patience and talking on a regular basis will help you find out what they are experiencing and how you can be supportive.

A third obstacle to family success is favoritism. In many cases, fathers who have children with whom they have visitation may, knowingly or unknowingly, treat them differently from the other children in the household. I mentioned that I initially showed some favoritism toward my daughter. I soon learned through the Biblical example of Joseph how extremely important it is not to do this. We all know how Joseph's brothers learned to hate him because of the favoritism shown by their father, and sold him into slavery. We can also clearly see through the life of Joseph how forgiveness, humility and obedience can bring life into wounded relationships.

In other instances, a woman may marry a man who has children, and later have a baby of her own. If not careful to continue developing these relationships, she can create the impression that the baby is all-important. It is also not uncommon that children who have grown up with a single parent have difficulty accepting a new person into these established relationships. Often they will try to put pressure between the husband and wife to get their natural parent to side with them. This is a kind of "coerced favoritism", playing on the parent's natural empathy for his or her child. However, if the husband and wife are aware of this tendency, they can agree on how to handle it and speak to it with a unified voice.

Another obstacle to be overcome may be your own feelings and mental images of a stepparent. The stepparent has been widely ridiculed in books and movies being portrayed as a mean, selfish individual who has no love or affection for the children. Many people view stepparents that way and this is totally unacceptable. We find in the scriptures that Jesus himself was raised by a stepfather.

The Bible says that Joseph was an honorable man who loved his wife and son, taught Jesus his trade as a carpenter and cared for him. You and I should take this example of what a stepparent should be, and learn that the term "step" does not have to denote distance, but rather a bridge of unity made between two people to facilitate healing and wholeness. We chose not to use the terms stepchild or stepparent in our family so that no one would feel less a part of the family than anyone else.

When you come into a marriage with children, you will have many feelings to work out. I will again use myself as the example of failing in the early years of parenting. When Lee and I married, I did not have full realization of the emotional commitment needed. I knew the financial commitment and responsibility well, but did not begin to comprehend the rejection I would feel from the children due to their own pain. I had no idea what was in store. I was not prepared to deal with the children at that stage. When they would say or do things that hurt my feelings, I had to learn that they were not necessarily trying to hurt my feelings, but that they were trying to handle their own hurt. In addition, when we were first married, I brought home a policeman's style of fathering. This was not only my chosen profession but also my view of the heavenly Father. I saw my Father God as someone up in heaven waiting for me to do something wrong so He could rebuke me and correct me. Of course, I learned He is not that at all. He is a loving, gracious, merciful, all-powerful, all-wise Father and I had some changing to do.

As I said, I initially brought some baggage into our relationship, not showing much compassion or mercy toward the boys, and showing some favoritism toward my daughter. I had visitation rights back then. I would pick up my daughter and spend weekends and days off with her and then take her back. It's natural for most fathers to be protective of their daughters and I had a difficult time taking her back after visits. When I went home, I expressed my anger, not with profanity but with hostility or sometimes, even opposition to our sons. I spoke to them roughly and handled them roughly at times. Again, they did nothing wrong to warrant this, and I had to repent of this wrong attitude and allow myself to be changed. I must reiterate that we can not blame our past for the way we act today. Yes, hurting people hurt people. However, as I yielded my life to the Lord, changes began to occur. Many of the walls in my life started to come down, one at a time.

From time to time, I would have angry emotional flare-ups, which we later found out by MRI were a result of brain damage from the chemical incident. For example, if I asked the boys to do something and they didn't do it the way I wanted it done, I would explode and treat them roughly, not being able to process stress and frustration in the normal way. I want to interject here that I was a volunteer prison chaplain for several years. One night while ministering to prisoners, unknown to them, they were also ministering to me. They were talking about how their fathers used to abuse them and how they still had unforgiveness in their hearts. They spoke of their need to CHOOSE TO FORGIVE their own fathers. When I went home from the prison, I knew that the next day, I had to do one of the most difficult things I had ever done. I sat with my sons and asked each of them to forgive me for my violent actions toward them. As I asked the Lord and my sons for forgiveness, healing began to take place in that part of our lives. They also made some changes as they understood the injury better and were glad to do so. After the verbal and physical abuse was dealt with and forgiven, the boys would tell you they understand and hold no grudges or bitterness toward me.

Communication of this kind is so important in every family. I ask fathers, especially, to plug into a local church, and other ministry resources like Christian TV and radio, and challenge yourself to grow. Show your family the reality of God's forgiveness. This situation showed our sons that I was teachable, able to grow through their forgiveness, and that I loved them enough to change.

Remember:
1. Children of divorce are wounded and angry too.
2. Affirm them often.
3. You can help them overcome with patience, understanding and encouragement.
4. Love them equally, but realize their needs are different.
5. Be willing to change.

PART II

Establishing A Home

The children's well-being on simple but important issues such as what name to call the new parent must be handled with care, and with the goal being long-lasting, happy family relationships. In our case, the three boys wanted to call me "Dad" but I was unable to handle that initially due to the hurt of not being able to raise my infant daughter. However, some years later, I realized that was wrong and selfish on my part. The boys, who are now grown men, continue to call me John but always refer to me as their Dad and we are very close. In my daughter's case, when she was four years old, she asked Lee if she could call her "Mom" and has done so ever since by her own choice.

The age of the children and closeness or lack of closeness to their birth parent must be a consideration on such a sensitive topic as this. No one should force any child to call a new parent Mom or Dad, but the more important objective is the mutual love and respect that each family member has for the other. The relationship that develops will dictate the terminology naturally.

My wife was the example of what a loving parent should be all through our marriage. She accepted my daughter as if she were her own. She also knew that the temper flares were not my personality but a result of the injury, and it was her way of addressing this issue that began the process of emotional healing. She confronted me just before the prisoners ministered to me that night. We discussed my temper and my treatment of our sons, and I knew I had to deal with these attitudes and actions. She said that although she knew it wasn't "me", she wasn't going to tolerate the behavior with no attempt to change. No, she never would have left me, but it was clear that the quality of our relationship would not have been the same if I didn't do something. I did not want to lose her or the children, the quality of love that we had or the future we wanted together. As I started to deal with this, she continued to love me and encourage me. She never nagged me. She always supported me when I would tell the children to be home at a particular time, for example, or that they could not go to a particular activity. There was never a question of division between us. The children knew that if I said something, she backed it up, and that's a good quality to have in any marriage. The same was true if she told the children to do something and I was not at home. They knew I supported her one hundred per cent. This kind of unity is so important to family life, and it helped me to conquer this problem and strengthen our relationships. Also, many potential problems were avoided because of the unity we maintain in our marriage.

Oh, Those Holidays!

A common problem in blended families is dealing with special holiday visits. How do you divide up holiday time for special visits? For many years as a police officer, I investigated domestic disputes pertaining to this type of problem. I realize there are usually court papers which must be considered in making holiday plans. In our family, we took the Biblical approach of meeting the needs of others first. As long as the children's well-being was not compromised, we enjoyed our holiday celebrations on alternate days, the most important thing being peace, togetherness and love in all relationships. Often times, there are parents who are not believers involved, and by using this approach, you sow seeds of God's love and also take tremendous pressure off the children. This helps bring healing to them as they see the demonstration of the love of

Christ to all, and are not forced to divide loyalty between parents.

School Days...

Let's discuss the making of decisions such as children's education. This issue must be thoroughly discussed and prayed over to make the right choice for each child. There are some fine public schools with some loving and caring teachers. Raising your family under the standard of the Word of God necessitates your involvement in the school system in a very intricate way. Be involved with your PTA but also research textbooks and subject matter, making sure they do not undercut your rights and responsibilities as a parent. If there are classes that are objectionable to you, you have the legal right (in New York State) to exclude your child from them. Others should research your state laws on this matter. This will take time and effort. Make sure you have ongoing conversations with teachers and with your children, staying on top of attitudes they may be learning. Be sure they are not learning disrespect, or ideas about making all their own choices at a very young age. Be sure to be teaching Biblical principles. Their attendance at church and youth groups should be faithful. A strong youth leader can help encourage the attitudes and moral values of your home.

Some families feel that Christian school is beyond their reach financially. We found that as we kept the principles of giving and tithing, we were able to send our children to private school and afford the tuition and uniforms while raising our family on half-pay. This decision must be weighed out carefully in each family. Every school, public or private, has its pluses and minuses. One school may be short on sporting activities but rate high in overall character building and academics. If the Christian school has some shortcomings but you decide to send your children there, find ways to supplement what you feel is lacking in the program.

Home schooling is another way of educating. Weigh it out. If you decide to home school as we did for our daughter's last three years of high school, make sure that you have particular guidelines and routines for them to follow. The children should have set times for working and be properly dressed for school so they don't become lax in their attitudes. Remember you are teaching life skills as well as schoolwork. It is also important to involve them in outside activities like dancing, sports, driver education, etc. Some school districts permit your students to be involved in school programs within your district. There are many wonderful options for home schoolers and organizations to help and support you if this is your choice.

As you discuss issues surrounding education, be open to each other, to new ideas and to resources in your community. Your decisions about schooling can bring you closer together or be divisive, depending on how you handle them. We decided to send our children to a Christian school when they ranged from third to twelfth grade. Being a senior in a public high school, our oldest son did not initially want to change schools, but we explained why we felt this was best for him. The advice to us was that it was too late in high school for him to benefit from transferring, but he did learn some valuable lessons while in the new school and benefited from some wonderful people. Make these decisions prayerfully and carefully according to your educational goals and purposes and the specific needs of your children.

Lead By Example

God's blueprint is for our children to be a blessing to us, which means a source of joy. Our family unit should be knit together with love, care and protection. However, many times this design is not being fulfilled. We, as parents, must begin with our own example. As we find words in the scriptures pertaining to the blessings and joys of children, we need to be the model first of what those words say. We need to demonstrate LEADERSHIP and the WILLINGNESS TO OBEY before we can tell our children to do likewise. One example is going to church on a weekly basis. (See Chapter 13) We must check our own attitude toward dress and authority so we can set consistent guidelines in the home for our children to follow. We must always be willing to BEGIN WITH OURSELVES. We must not be content to live a double standard, telling our children what is right and good but demonstrating something less. We may have to repent and ask forgiveness in this area if we have been living a double standard in front of our children, but it's never too late to do what's right. Don't let guilt or condemnation stop you. Then, make simple changes.

Start to attend church with a proper attitude. Create a wholesome environment in your home. Men, pray with your wives and children. There has been a great controversy for several decades over having prayer in the public schools, and rightfully so. There should be opportunity for prayer. However, PRAYER IN THE HOME is not outlawed. We have seen through many in the scripture – Abraham, Noah, David, Joseph – the effect of making an altar. Daniel made an altar while in captivity in Babylon. You and I can start making an altar in our homes, simply meaning making a time and place for prayer and thanksgiving with our families every day. Be faithful to this time and place of prayer, speaking the Word of God, teaching your children that they have purpose, value and gifts from God, and that it's His desire to make them whole. Our children need to know that they have great worth, that God has a plan for them and He is concerned about everything that concerns them. They need to know

111

that part of their purpose right now is going to school, being involved in healthy activities with other young people, and preparing for the future. Taking responsibilities around the home and eventually a part-time job will help prepare them for adult life. We need to remember that an effective parent teaches the children a good work ethic, a proper attitude toward responsibility, accountability to God and family and eventually, to society.

When our children become teen-agers, our culture will tell them that they are their own persons and can do whatever they want. I disagree! Again, the Word is our blueprint. No one has the right to do whatever he wants; we are all accountable. We must teach our young people that MATURITY AND INDEPENDENCE DO NOT NECESSARILY EQUATE WITH AGE, but rather with BEHAVIOR AND RESPONSIBILITY. Use simple, practical ways to teach responsibility, like assigning age-appropriate chores, and be sure that they are accomplished. Determine to develop better communication. Institute after supper discussions, as an example. These can be informal talks about events, problems, Biblical solutions and prayer.

Let me add that children's rooms are not off-limits to parents. As a policeman, I went into homes where the parents did not go into their teens' rooms because they were "his or her space". This concept is wrong. That room is part of your house. You may give them some freedom to decorate it or furnish it tastefully in a way that meets with your approval, but that does not mean that anything goes. On many of these calls, there would be music, weapons, drugs or other items that would have a harmful effect on the young person's attitude and mindset. We would have to carefully remove these individuals from the home when the parents would call because they had lost control.

We must determine not to operate with this type of attitude. We must explain to our teens what our expectations are. They may not understand or like it at first but the principle is not up for discussion. Explain that you are not going to be a policeman in your home, but you expect the room to be clean and free from objectionable materials. Explain what the standard is. In this sense, the child's room is no different from any other room in the house. What is not permitted in the house is not permitted in the child's room. Keep in touch with who their friends are, what they watch and listen to, and what comes into your home. That's not spying, that's caring! You will spare your children heartache and keep your family from being scattered. That is God's will and purpose for all families. Every member should be able to talk, be heard, and have respect, responsibility and latitude. Responsibilities and privileges change as children grow and demonstrate various stages of maturity. This is a process that does not stop at any particular age, no matter how long your children live at home. Look at every obstacle as an opportunity to build character and to meet the unique needs and challenges of your family. There are also wonderful rewards ahead. The deep bonds and lasting relationships that develop in spite of how you may begin are deeply fulfilling and satisfying.

Establishing Our Home Environment

A couple needs to recognize that their home is like a fort or a haven for all family members in which to enjoy SAFE AND PEACEFUL SURROUNDINGS. A peaceful home, in some cases, does not come overnight. By our example and by teaching our family why we are making certain changes, we can create a more peaceful atmosphere. An example might be that certain types of music or television programs simply are not permissible. There must be a standard of expected behavior and certain attitudes that will not be tolerated. There are no double standards for the children, whether they live with you all the time or come over for days, weekends or vacations. All children will be loved and cared for and the rules of the home apply to all. There might be a season of seeming unrest or attitudes that bring disharmony into the home. You must not allow this to affect the marriage relationship, and you must be firm in your decision to maintain a peaceful home. You simply must not allow attitudes that are often displayed in the public arena to reign in your home. Children do not have a right to make final decisions and have the last word over their parents. We should always listen to their needs and problems and be compassionate, but we must also live in God's order. Children have a right to be loved and nurtured in the way of the Lord and a responsibility to come under the parents' authority in the home. They will do this as long as we remain faithful and recognize where their attitudes are coming from. We must teach them that certain attitudes (which they may be learning outside of the home) do not meet the Godly standard by which we choose to live. As they recognize that this peaceful home is for their best long-term good, the choices will be clear. Give them opportunities to dialogue with you, but there must always be ground rules – speaking with respect, no yelling, no swearing, no raised voices, for example. Children often see this kind of disrespectful behavior toward parents and others in authority portrayed in the media and among friends. You must make perfectly clear what is and is not acceptable in your home. As stated before, there might be a season of disharmony over this, but keep your focus on the long-term goal, and be persistent. If children do not learn to respect authority at home, they will neither respect God's authority nor be able to function successfully in adult society.

All Things New

Begin your own family traditions. Celebrate birthdays and holidays with enthusiasm and creativity. Include grandparents and extended family as often as possible. Be loving and compassionate in your discipline. Establish your family as a team with a strong unity between husband and wife. Give your children guidance. Have family meetings to discuss problems and possible solutions. Be open and honest and always use the Word of God as your blueprint. Teach and demonstrate a good work ethic. All children should have age-appropriate responsibilities and then privileges as they prove faithful to their tasks. Teach your sons and daughters to cook, clean, shop, do laundry, cut grass and keep the home and yard. Remember, it's not just today's job for today, but TODAY'S ATTITUDE FOR TOMORROW! You are equipping your sons and daughters to go off to school, to work or to a new family someday. A young husband who knows what his wife handles at home can have greater understanding and input. Young women should not feel helpless either in handling some things usually reserved for men, like grass cutting or fixing minor things around the house and yard. As your children develop a sense of responsibility, they will appreciate more the time they have for recreation. Our children will survive change if we are faithful, compassionate and demonstrate unity, in the process of life changes. It's what they learn now, even if it's only two or three years under our roof, that can provide the foundation for their adulthood.

Remember:
1. Confront issues lovingly.
2. Put the needs of others first.
3. Maturity and independence equate with behavior and responsibility.

4. Lead by example.
5. Begin your own family traditions.
6. Cultivate today's attitude for tomorrow.

PART III

A Higher Standard

As stated before, there is a real attempt to take away parental authority and to erode Biblical rights and responsibilities of parents. We are to instruct and demonstrate to our children by our lifestyle that there are consequences to our actions. Therefore, each home needs to have rules or guidelines. If we take the Word as our example, we see that our Heavenly Father gave us rules. They are not suggestions, but commandments which are still the basis of all moral law established for the good of man. Our nation was founded on these rules, and we can see the destruction as we stray from these guidelines. An example of this is the modern-day teaching that we are to be our children's friends. Our four children now range in age from twenty-two to thirty-one years of age. Yes, they are our friends, but we did not make decisions based on the concept that we wanted them to be our friends. We worked at parenting. Friendships came later as they matured. God gave us the responsibility and privilege of giving our family a home where His values would be lived out and shape the character of our children. If we forsake parenting for friendship, we raise unhappy, disconnected young people who don't know how to relate to "Father God" or to other authority figures. We handicap their development and cripple their ability to have successful relationships because they don't know how to submit to anyone on the one hand, or how to properly exercise authority on the other. It's more important to raise them in the values we wish them to internalize as they mature than to treat them as friends now. Friends are peers. Our children will not be our peers until they are adults, and even then, we will have a special relationship with them that both underscores and transcends the friendship.

They are more likely to enjoy friendship with us if they have known us as stable, consistent "real" parents – able to admit when we're wrong, to laugh and have fun and to set important boundaries that protect them from harm.

Through the process, don't allow your family to be unduly pressured by outside influences. I found, for example, that many people have unreal expectations of what the family of a policeman or a minister should be like. Our families are expected to be perfect with no one ever making a mistake or a wrong choice. Of course, this is unrealistic and unhealthy. As we entered the ministry, we had to guard our family against the pressure of other people's attitudes. We explained to our children that, like it or not, we would be looked to as examples. We did not expect perfection from each other, but we all needed to think before we made choices. If we made some choices that turned out to be wrong, we would continue to go back to the foundation of forgiveness, make corrections and then go on with our lives. I encourage readers who are in ministry, or who are highly visible for other reasons, to operate in this way, not letting others put undue pressure on your family.

As mentioned before, it was important for our children to know that we would not be divided over issues. If my wife or I made a decision for the children, the other was supportive and the children soon learned that they would not get a different answer to the same question from the other parent. If I was too hard on them, and as I said there was a season when I was, my wife did not change my decision. We would talk in private and then I would have an opportunity to explain my decision to the children and change it if appropriate. This was a growing experience for all of us. Our children were also taught that I only expected from them what I gave them first. I spoke to them with honesty and no hidden agenda, and I weighed out my decisions focusing on the long term. My goal was to raise our family in the love and the ways of God so that as adults, they would be skillful in the Word, and their decisions would be guided by the principles taught and modeled in our home.

Teach By Example

The blended family offers unique opportunities and challenges in parenting children who are not siblings by birth, whether they are together all the time or only on weekends and vacations. It must be recognized that what is allowed into the home is extremely important, from music and TV programs to friends and activities. We can't tell our children not to watch certain types of movies and then bring them home and watch them when the children are not around. This type of double standard will come back to haunt us. We have to LIVE THE STANDARD in front of them to be taken seriously by our children. All parents must say what they mean and mean what they say. For example, when I was a working officer, I did not consume alcohol because I believed it was wrong for me to do so as a public servant in the trust of the people. I had investigated many traffic fatalities and alcohol-related crimes and saw the effects of its use. I could not arrest someone for driving while intoxicated and then go off-duty and drink. I brought this conviction into parenting as well and would not tell our children to do anything that I was not living myself.

The home should be a place where all the family can come from work, school or activities, hang their hats, be relaxed and not be afraid they will be laughed at or mocked. This is everyone's place to be themselves, have choices of good activity and productive interactions. As everyone makes daily choices, the "ultimate choice" – God and His way – is always part of our discussions. As your children grow, they will see that you are STABLE AND

CONSTANT. They will know that you mean what you say and that they can count on your word.

Moms and Dads, guard your homes and be careful what you let in. I once tried to stop a car for a routine vehicle and traffic infraction. A high-speed chase ensued and the car I was pursuing hit a telephone pole and was cut in half. The youth who drove the car was not seriously injured. Upon arrest, I asked him why he ran from me. He answered that he saw them do it on TV all the time. Every time there was a television movie which portrayed crime as very appealing or demonstrated the mechanics of a crime, within a few days we would see copy-cat crimes. These might be thefts, burglaries or even violent crimes. Don't let anyone tell you that television does not have a tremendous influence upon its viewers. There would not be so much money in advertising if that were true.

Today the violence and lack of morals on television is greater than when our children were small and it needs to be monitored very carefully, as do other things that come into the home. Don't be intimidated by friends who still allow a loose moral life style to influence their homes. Take the courage and time you need to make good changes. Explain them to your children as you go, remembering that younger children can make changes more easily than older ones. Teens need a little more time to adapt and more family discussions to help them do so. Take time to explain that even though they may have done some of these things in the past, you believe that the new way is the best course for the whole family. Talk to them, bring them into discussions, but don't allow their feelings to divide you or to play favorites between parents. This is especially important in blended families. Children often attempt to "butter up" one parent or the other. Don't let it work in your home.

Once decisions were made in our home, they stuck unless there was some very good reason to change them.

Our rules were few and simple. We lived and expected scriptural attitudes like integrity, honesty and willingness to help others. As our children learned to make decisions, they would come to me and explain their goals and I would help them form a sound choice. Gradually, they took on more of the process, but always came for a final approval while living at home.

There's Safety and Wisdom in Numbers

I tried to be flexible in giving the children opportunities to enjoy group social activities, especially in the company of people of good moral character. Lee and I made a decision at one point that our children would not be involved in the typical dating scene, pairing off at an early age and having romantic attachments. We believe that if we allowed our children to go along with the flow of dating, we would have exposed them to the pain and hurt of emotional involvement and too many choices before they were ready. We made this decision when our sons were young teens, explaining our Bible responsibility as parents to exercise wisdom in this regard for their sakes. They did try to understand. After discussion, they followed our advice without any major problems. They had an adjustment period but it was one of cordial understanding. We reinforced to them that this was a decision in their own interest to save them from hurt feelings and heartache which many teens go through when encouraged to date from an early age. As they saw some of their friends get involved in relationships that were unhealthy, counter-productive or that actually took them off course in life, they understood. It wasn't too long before they began to share with friends that it was best to listen to their parents on this issue. We are not referring to proms, youth groups, church socials or concerts where our young people can get to know each other in groups with adult supervision. Remember, young people need to be taught what it means to be Godly men and women so they need to be around some! If your children are already dating, it's not too late to add some guidelines and boundaries if you have not done so already. You might want to rethink this and make sure there is open communication with your children. Be sure you know where and with whom they are spending their time. God will give you wisdom. I am convinced of the old saying "If we involve ourselves in prevention, we will do less intervention". Make sure when you allow your children to date that they are not getting in over their heads. Every child does not have the same maturity at the same age. God is full of mercy, healing and great wisdom so let's use all the wisdom we can gain.

"Mother, May I..."

In addition to dating, children are often allowed to make too many decisions for themselves at too young an age. They are often exposed to unhealthy influences simply because they are not mature enough to make certain choices, but are allowed to make them anyway. Often young people choose their own music, dress, friends and entertainment without restriction. Many of them also have a good bit of money to spend as they wish. Remember, young people are specifically targeted in so much of the media regarding alcohol, lust and perversion. We have counseled parents, some of whom are in the ministry, who have raised their families with this kind of freedom of choice. Some of these parents have come to us with adult children in the prison system because they thought they could make any choices they wished. Some used to say that I was too strict, but time proved the need for limiting choices. The balance here is from the scripture, not legalism or the other extreme either, where children can dress and act any way they wish and dictate to the parents what they will do and where they will go. This is not correct nor is it loving parenting. We are mandated by God to use His Word as a standard, to promote what is right, and not to be afraid to be ridiculed by others, even in the church. Remember, your family's future is at stake.

Constructive Disagreements

All children will disagree from time to time. We began to teach our children at a very early age how to talk through their difficulties with each other and not to hold bitterness or resentment. After talking among themselves, if apologies needed to be made, they were made. They also told each other they loved one another and hugged after differences were settled. They were to realize that God gave them to each other and that they had great purpose together. They were never to leave unfinished business on a negative note, making room for unforgiveness.

Along this line, we had a rule in our house which had to do with the sharing of gifts, toys or other belongings. It went like this. "If you can't share it, you can't have it." If the children placed a higher value on any "thing" than on a brother or sister with whom it could be shared, that particular thing had to be set aside so they could reflect on their values. The fruit of this has been immeasurable. It might not be a bad idea to do this among adults!

In the long run, children need to know that they will not be thrown away if they make a mistake or a wrong decision. All situations can be worked out with patience, forgiveness and a Godly standard. It's important how we handle the times when they make decisions that go against their upbringing. As an example, one of our sons went to Bible college out of state. As I mentioned, the financing was a sacrifice at that time due to my injury, but the Lord provided the funds. During his second year at school, he called home and said he wanted to marry a particular girl.

He had wanted to marry a couple of times previously, so my objection to his marrying was not based on the girl, but on the fact that he was not yet ready for marriage. Time did bear me out on this. Our son was some fifteen hundred miles from home and he was determined to get married. Even though I knew that this timing was not correct, he decided against my advice. In fact, he had pastors call me to say that he could make the choice he wanted. That was true, but let me remind you that just because an individual is of legal age (or even has gray hair!) does not mean that he or she is doing the right thing. A praying parent knows when a major decision like this is proper for his or her child.

Our son did get married in another state while Lee and the other two boys were out of the country on a short-term mission trip. Needless to say, it was stressful for both families. I felt there needed to be some time and distance between us, so there was a period of about six months when I did not have communication with him. One day the Holy Spirit dropped into my heart to call our son, whose wife was not from this part of the country, and invite them up for Christmas. Yes, you heard right! I was obedient and called. (Our son recently told us how shocked he was when he got that phone call!) I sent them two tickets and, practically speaking, I didn't have the money. They came home for two weeks at Christmas and we met our beautiful new daughter-in-law for the first time. It was not the girl that was wrong. The Lord used Lee and me to save their marriage at times, to help them grow, and I am pleased to say they have been married for some eleven years now. They have given us four beautiful grandchildren and they have a good marriage. However, they went through some heartaches between then and now which they realize could have been prevented.

When our children asked my advice, I always gave it. If they took it, that was fine. If they chose not to and made a decision which they later regretted, I never said "I told you so!" I chose to love them through that period of adjustment. After our daughter graduated from high school, she wanted to enroll in Bible school. Just before school began, she ran away from home. Some wrong ideas about me had been planted in her mind and since she had just turned eighteen, others were telling her that she could make her own choices and do what she wanted. I caution all parents not to be so free with their advice. Trying to take over a parent's responsibility is something that needs to be dealt with delicately. Parents who serve the Lord and have raised their children will have a foundation for decision-making, and are best equipped to help their children with important matters.

When she ran away, we did not feel the Lord had let us down or that His Word was not true. It's not what happens to you in life, but HOW YOU RESPOND TO IT that makes the difference. Yes, we were upset, we cried, we were hurt. Those are normal feelings in situations like that. We prayed and searched our hearts. What we did not do was just as important as what we did. WE DID NOT BLAME our daughter, her friends or anyone else. Yes, this was an attempt to divide our family, but the scripture is true, "...no weapon that is formed against you will prosper" (Is. 54:17). WE DID NOT COMPLAIN. We did not blame God or act hopelessly in this matter, because our faith was not in our feelings or in what appeared to be so.

Many parents today do not know where their children are. I would encourage them by saying that when we did not know where our daughter was, the Lord knew where she was. He knows where your children are right now. Continue praying and believing; continue thanking Him. During this time, we had several ministry dates previously booked and we did not cancel them. We felt that to do so would take us far off course and we would not accomplish

God's will. We continued to meet the needs of others believing that God would take care of our situation.

While she was gone from home, we continued to minister to others out of our own hurt and pain, but never out of a hopeless spirit. One evening while watching Tri-State Christian Television, a telethon was being aired to raise funds for the coming year. You may wonder what this had to do with our daughter's returning home. Here is how the Lord worked. A minister was preaching from Ephesians 6:8 on the theme that what we make happen for others, God will make happen for us when we do not have the ability to do it for ourselves. In other words, we could not speak to our daughter. We could not tell her that we loved her and that God loved her, yet we could let others know of God's love through television. We pledged an amount of money to the station and sent off the check. No, you do not buy God's favor, but by faith, acting out of the prodding of the Holy Spirit, we planted a seed of faith as God directed us. By supporting this ministry, other children away from home would be able to hear of the love of God by means of the broadcast. As we sent the check, we believed that God would bring our daughter home soon. We didn't know how long she would be gone, but the very next day we found out where she was and within forty-eight hours she was home. God's wisdom, His mercy and our obedience are powerful in our circumstances. We never said "I told you so". In fact, she later wrote about this event in a term paper, explaining that it was a great learning and growing experience for her. It turned out to be that for all of us.

Mountain, Move!

Let me encourage you right now not to let decisions like these "handcuff" you. What I mean by that is that when a family member goes through a valley, you must stay in the Word of God, the will of God and the way of God. Yes, you will hurt, you will be frustrated and you might not even know where they are at times. You might live in a home situation where there is a lot of strife, but you must continually speak the words of God in your home. When your loved ones are not at home, go into their rooms and lay hands on their beds or pillows and pray a believing prayer. Pray that the Holy Spirit will make a breakthrough with your child, that there will be peace instead of strife and confusion in their hearts. Prayers like that work!

Some people refer to the need for family devotions. In our home, every mealtime is an occasion to share spiritual food. The Word of God mandates that we live the life and teach our children through all experiences. Part of that teaching is seeing us handle life experiences each and every day. How do we pay our bills? How do we give to the Lord and to others? How do we keep a home? How do we treat one another? The family's devotions must be more than structured teachings, in fact must be a life style of teaching. Relate the day's activities to the principles of the Word at all times (Deut. 6:5-7). This life teaching will help your children learn to make decisions in line with God's principles for themselves.

Enjoy your family. If you are going through difficulties right now, you can enjoy knowing that God loves you, that His Word is true and that as long as you continue to focus on His goodness and mercy, THIS TOO SHALL PASS! You might have to go for counseling to help work out some problems. You might even have to go to some legal authorities if there is violent behavior in the home. Your son or daughter might be in jail. There is tremendous revival going on in our prison system right now, so be thankful that you know where they are. Be thankful that they are in a prime location to come to the Lord in a real way. Even though they might have had knowledge before, this is an opportunity for them to experience the love and mercy of God and He will prove Himself to your children. Remember, God has no grandchildren. Each must come on his own.

If your children make decisions against the Word and their upbringing, don't over react. Determine to be joyful. Love them to wholeness. Be thankful even at times when you are upset and crying. Have hope – not the kind the world offers, but hope in the living God and His promises. Don't turn against each other, parents. Don't blame each other for the particular way a child is growing up. Keep your focus on God's goodness even though it might take a season to work these things out. Time, in God's perspective, is different from ours.

The good seed you've sown in their lives is never wasted. Don't tell your children that they are rebellious or good for nothing. Refuse to speak negatively to them. Start today to speak words of encouragement, words that they will line up with eventually, words of hope and promise. Speak words that God can bless and fulfill. That's faith.

Remember:
1. Live the standard in front of your children.
2. Limit your children's choices.
3. Support your children through poor decisions and help them change.
4. Stay on course.
5. This too shall pass!

PART IV

Attitude Is Everything

It is God's will for parents to have an eternal effect on their children. This starts with prayer and the study of God's Word, and the application of those principles to every day life. If you want to see change, do not allow your "natural eye" to discourage you from believing God to move in your life and circumstances. Speak words of faith and encouragement to your children, and over them, no matter what age they are or in what situations they are. They might live under your roof or far away, or you might not know where they are right now. Make simple changes and faithfully apply them on a daily basis. Develop a spirit of praise and thanksgiving and speak what the Lord wants your family to be – whole, unified, and fulfilling its purpose and destiny. Each member of your family can reach goals in life if we learn to view them through "eyes of faith", and encourage them according to God's plan – "calling those things which be not as though they were" (Romans 4:17).

Husbands, I encourage you to take your wife's hand and ask the Lord for His wisdom, His guidance, His protection and His love. Taking her hand in prayer may be foreign to you, but don't let that stop you. Just start where you are. It might be a few minutes before you go to work. Ask God's protection on all of you while you're away from each other and then build on that. Pray with your children before they leave for school. As you go to work, listen to the Bible on tape or to Christian radio. There is a wealth of material on tape that can help encourage your growth, and what better time to utilize it than on the way to work. There are good teaching tapes by Godly men and women available at local book stores that can speak life into you, not to mention uplifting music that can put you on a higher plane in spirit before you ever get to an on-the-job problem. This will build up your inner self and in turn, your spouse will be built up. Encouraging one another will make you more apt to encourage your children, and be better equipped to handle their needs. These principles are timeless and powerful. What you are allowing to occur is the OPENING OF YOUR HEART AND HOME TO THE HOLY SPIRIT – to His Word, His attributes and His favor.

For many years now, we have enjoyed the times when our family is all together. When all our children were at home, Lee and I instituted times of talking with each other about the things of God and how to apply them to our lives. We encouraged our children to talk about issues that interested them. That might be anything from school and friends to relationships or current events. What this did as they were growing up was to develop in them the ability to communicate, and a sense of how to handle problems that we all face. They learned that we do not run from problems or feelings, but we do not live out of them either. We live from the Word of God and talk through and work through difficulties openly. We always began with prayer, giving each one the opportunity to pray. These times need not be long and should be filled with joy and hope, and a spirit of praise and thanks. It could be after supper, just a "spontaneous" event, when you might share a verse of scripture you read that day or a principle you think your family needs to learn about. This is an excellent way to teach your family and share your own experiences with them while making the precepts real to them in an informal setting. It brings home the reality that God cares for us, not only on Sundays, but every day. Demonstrate a spirit of unity and agreement during these times. Lee and I also shared what we were going through and how the children could pray for us, and we would pray for any situation they brought to the table. In doing these things, you deposit in your sons and daughters the image of what an excellent marriage under the Lord is all about. Don't despise small beginnings!

You might say, "John, my spouse won't pray with me". Then start by yourself. God is not a respecter of persons. Invoke the covenant of God – in other words, His Word over your life. Determine to be obedient to Him. By doing so, your character will change and your faith will take root in the specific promises of God. Your influence on your spouse and family will become greater as you appropriate those promises. Don't be discouraged; God is on your side. Your family will not only survive but become stronger under the influence of your prayers. Ask God to change your spouse's attitude about praying together, but don't nag. It's a lot easier to respond positively to the Holy Spirit than to nagging!

We have done this from the beginning, and now that our children are grown, we still get together and have these special times. They also call on us to agree with them in prayer when problems arise in their lives or the lives of relatives and friends.

In order for life to be fulfilling and powerful, it needs to be steeped in prayer. There are volumes written on the subject, so just let me say that it is not complicated. Prayer is simply pouring your heart out honestly to God and awaiting His response. Just start with the basic understanding that God loves you, He wants to converse with you, and He has written you a love letter in the form of His Word. Often we only cry out to God in a crisis, and out of His awesome faithfulness, He answers us. But we can develop a spirit of prayer, praise and thanks by growing in our relationship with Him daily. Simply talk to Him out loud, thank Him even before you request anything, and realize that without God you are going nowhere. Your family might be going through upheaval, and you might have lived by a double standard in the past. You may feel ill-equipped to manage your children's problems.

Determine that from this moment on, things are going to be different. As Joshua said, "As for me and my house, we will serve the Lord" (Joshua 24:15b). It only takes one person holding fast to the Lord and to His promises to make a big difference. Stay in prayer and in faith and don't compromise the principles you are determined to live and teach. Worship Him and allow Him to direct you.

CHILDREN WILL LEARN WHAT THEY LIVE AT HOME. They need to know that there are definite consequences to their actions, which should be known ahead of time and anticipated. The consequence should be proportionate to the offence and carried out when necessary. Keep the rules few and simple. When our children broke the rules, I learned to tell them I would carry out the discipline in a little while and would handle the matter when I had a cool head. I'd always hug them afterward and tell them that they were not the problem, but their actions were wrong. Whether your children need a stern talking to or privileges taken away, learn not to discipline in anger, but in love. Remind them that you love them so that the discipline produces the desired effect.

Parenting Parents

If you are fortunate enough to have your parents still living, continue to show love and respect to them and include them in your family life as much as possible. You may be caring for their needs as they age, much as you cared for the needs of your children. This is not uncommon today, and I encourage you to spend some time with your aging parents if possible. No matter what the relationship was in the past, you have the opportunity to bless them now. Even if you were abused or wronged, God's grace and mercy are sufficient for all, and you may bring healing and wholeness into what is left of their lives. Show respect for your parents in any case. If they live far from you, phone calls and cards can be loving communication, not just at holidays but often. By showing them respect, you are also teaching your children to respect their parents.

Be Flexible

The scripture teaches us not to provoke our children to anger, and this sometimes occurs through a legalistic, inflexible approach to parenting (Ephesians 6:4). The Word of God is balanced, bringing the commandments for living on the one hand and His grace and mercy on the other. God wants you and your family to be whole and living in that balance. Don't be so rigid that you can't ADMIT A MISTAKE or try something new. Don't be so wishy-washy that you have no convictions about things that should not be compromised. God wants you to plant seeds of goodness and love in your sphere of influence beginning with your family, so let His Word be the rule of thumb in your home and His love, the prevailing attitude.

Conclusion

The establishment of a Biblical pattern and some "new' family traditions will give all members of the family security, order and stability. No matter where you live, peace and contentment will follow that order and stability. Refuse to blame your past or others who have hurt you, and determine to deal with yourself before God and take responsibility for your actions. If there is some resistance to change in your home initially, be faithful, compassionate and demonstrate unity with your spouse, and you will achieve the long-term life changes you are looking for.

Remember that contentment is resting in the Lord. We all want to spare our children the hurt and disappointment in life that we have suffered. Often, we take on guilt and condemnation in the child-raising process. As we learn to rest in God and develop eyes of faith and an attitude of prayer, we will handle crises better and not be so easily shaken. As we replace worry and concern with prayer and thanksgiving, we sense God's power in our midst. Contentment is knowing that it is God's will for us to be made whole and realizing that He has given us the tools and resources to see it accomplished.

You can live in this peace no matter what is going on around you. Learn to enjoy your relationship with God, your spouse and your children. Don't place unrealistic expectations on yourselves or on each other. Learn to laugh and cry together. As you do, you will develop the intimacy and deep trust that we all desire in our relationships.

Our children ranged in age from four to thirteen years old when we married almost eighteen years ago. We have all gained a deeper love and appreciation for one another and our children still come to me for advice! There is a deep joy and reward in seeing your children and your grandchildren walk in the ways of the Lord. We all go through difficult seasons, but we must look through the eyes of faith, not our feelings, in this critical area of raising children.

Remember:
1. Maintain unity with your spouse.
2. Children learn what they live at home.
3. Be willing to admit when you are wrong.
4. Discipline with love, not anger.
5. Rest in God.

CHAPTER ELEVEN

PARENTING FROM A DISTANCE

It is the will of God that we parent with integrity. Not being able to live with your children is very difficult for all involved. If allowed to be, this process of parenting from a distance can be an emotional roller coaster. You may be faced with feelings of guilt, failure and rejection. Attitudes of anger, bitterness and resentment, if allowed to persist, can devastate you for years to come. Obviously, you can not go back, but you can have solid, peaceful and long-term loving relationships with your children and be a productive parent by yielding yourself to the Lord and the principles of His Word. Integrity, faithfulness and involvement in their lives will go a long way toward accomplishing this goal.

Being a person of character and integrity simply means making decisions that are best for the children, remembering that you want to be intricately involved in the decision-making process concerning them throughout their growing-up years. You want to plant seeds of the mercy and love of God and the power of His healing. An example of this in my own life was the decision not to relocate to another police department after I divorced. I had ample opportunity to relocate, and many people advised me to do so in order to put away my past and go on with my life. However, I did not yield to my feelings at that time, considering the love I had for my daughter and the need she would have for my love as she was growing up. I submitted myself to a better course of action by staying.

My first four and half years of parenting was in the role of a single father with visitation. My infant daughter was approximately six months old at the time, and I was not a believer for the first year and a half. I still chose the path that would give her the best care I could assure in the situation. I went beyond the legal obligations, not only for my daughter's care but also for her mother, recognizing that if I could help her, it might also produce a better environment in which to raise her. There were many times that I could have acted out of hurt, anger or other negative emotions I was experiencing. However, if I had done that, my long-term objective of being able to give my daughter a good home would have been ruined. Taking matters into your own hands, no matter how justified it may seem, is not the proper response when you have children living in an unhealthy environment. As a police officer, I could have done this and justified the actions, but I chose another path trying to help the situation as much as I could.

After my conversion, there was still almost a three-year period of being a single father. I had mercy, grace and forgiveness operating in me, and I began to deposit these into my little girl's life. Because she was approximately eighteen months old, you might wonder what I could do at that stage of her life. Being faithful to her on my two days off each week was very important to both of us. I worked rotating shifts, but chose not to work second jobs or socialize on those days off. I looked forward to picking her up every week. I had moved back home with my mother at that time which gave her a stable home to come to on a regular basis. Although as a single parent I felt this situation had shortcomings, I realized that I could only be a father, not a mother. My mother stepped in and fulfilled the role of a loving grandmother, helping us through this period of our lives.

Being a person of integrity means recognizing your past failures, dealing with them in the Lord, and choosing a life that will be peace-making in situations that can be very stressful. I was faithful to my daughter. I would call her, send cards, drop off little things for her – not trying to buy her love – but just showing concern for her as a father should. Also, I chose not to argue or have disagreements in front of her. It's not healthy for children to be subjected to bickering or unproductive communication. They have enough insecurity already. You can make appropriate opportunities to discuss important matters, but choose to do so in a peaceful manner and do not let your emotions take over.

Fathers, Do Not Provoke Your Children

Dads especially, do not manhandle young children that are under your care and supervision. You're probably dealing with frustration as it is, so find a proper vent for it. Keep in mind that children will need to be corrected, but in the proper way. Manhandling will only serve to put a distance between you and your children, and to provoke them to anger, which they have no proper way to vent. They may also begin to fear you, and bottle up this fear and anger for a later time. If this kind of handling persists, by the time they are ten or twelve years old, they may begin to shove back, having learned that this is the way to handle anger, frustration and disappointment. They may also learn to be violent with others, and we've seen enough evidence of that. Men need to be especially aware of not being heavy-handed with children.

Let's use the example of picking up your children on a regular basis and taking them to church. This is a very good idea if you are able to do so, but remember, your church environment may be foreign to them. They may not know what to expect. Take them as regularly as you can and perhaps you can take them a little early and explain what will occur and what behavior is expected of them. Talk to Sunday school teachers too, especially if your children are there on a less than regular basis. Keep them abreast of your children's needs, and they will probably be willing to go an extra mile to make the church experience a happy and fulfilling one. If your children are sitting with you in services, I strongly suggest you provide Bible coloring books or other age-appropriate activities to help span the long periods that are not geared to their attention. It's difficult for a child to sit through an adult service, and you want their association with church and God to be a pleasant one, not a hassle. Hopefully, they will want to come to church, and as they enjoy their classroom activities, you are building love and joy into them through the ministry of the local church.

Should your child display an inappropriate behavior like coloring on the walls, for example, don't over react. This is not a reflection of you. Dad, make sure you have dealt with or are dealing with your own hurt and rejection so that you are not taking your frustration out on your child. As you deal with these things in the Lord, you will gain better control of your emotions. It is important to DISCIPLINE WITHOUT ANGER. Getting back to the child coloring on the walls, make sure you spend a few minutes by yourself to cool off. Don't grab the child in anger, but take his or her hand in yours and sit alone, explaining what went wrong. If the behavior warrants further discipline at home, be sure it is FAIR AND PRIVATE so the child is not humiliated in front of others or hurt physically. Loss of privileges is very effective in changing behavior. Be sure to hug your child and tell him that you love him. Let him know that he is not bad, but the behavior choice was bad. Do not give the impression that you love him only when he's well behaved.

You must lovingly discipline, never in anger or rage. Don't always pick out the negatives in your child's behavior either. Many of the things children do are done just because they are children, not because they are bad. They need love, instruction and good examples. If you spend fun time with your children, you will spend less time disciplining. Make church fun. This might be their only opportunity to come into contact with other Christians. Be sure to provide a balance in the love of God to your children. Hug them often Dad, and tell them you love them. Provide appropriate activities to help them through long waiting periods. Don't be concerned about what other people think. They are not in your shoes. Just be consistent in planting seeds that will reap a Godly harvest. Don't forget, it was the love of God that drew us to Him.

The same applies if you have older children or teens. When they go to church with you, be thankful they are there. If they need to be corrected, do so in a proper manner by talking with them and loving them into new ways. As they get involved in youth activities whenever possible, even if it's only once or twice a month, this is still good sowing.

You might wonder if it's worth the trouble of taking your children to church every other weekend. Let me share a situation that will encourage you. I had a close brother in the Lord who was divorced with two small children. He would travel an hour one way every other weekend to pick up his children and an hour back to his residence. Every other weekend, these children were in Sunday school, church activities, vacation Bible school in the summers, and special holiday events. There was not a friendly relationship between the Mom and Dad, but the Lord prepared the hearts of both parents so that they agreed this was best for the children. (Don't leave God out of these decisions!) This occurred year after year. When the children were about fourteen and fifteen, their Dad became ill and went to be with the Lord a short time later. Those young people stood up and thanked their father, the congregation, Sunday school teachers and pastors for the acceptance and love that was planted in their lives all those years. That's what they remembered about their Dad. He loved God and he loved them, and he showed it by his acts of kindness and faithfulness to them through that local church. They are young adults now with a foundation in faith, love and mercy, and God's Word. Parents, it's worth the trials, tribulations, and at times, aggravations to plant deeply within our children. Go the extra mile.

House Rules

Having a spouse to aid you in this child-raising period of your life is an immeasurable blessing. The previous discussion of unity between husband and wife is all-important here to maximize the limited time with your visiting children. You and your spouse need to be in agreement ahead of time on the rules of your home that will apply to all your children. There can not be a double standard of behavior and expectation for children who live at home and those who visit. If a particular child is allowed more choices when he or she is not with you, it must be understood that the rules of your home still apply to all, to avoid misunderstanding or the perception of favoritism. Explain to the children that out of your love and concern and commitment to God, these are the rules that all family members will embrace. KEEP THE RULES FEW AND SIMPLE. This will allow for a smoother transition even for teens, and will not bring division in the long run, but strength.

Dads, if there are occasions when the children need discipline, do not take the children's side against your wife. If she has determined that such action is appropriate, support her and it will be seen that there will not be division or favoritism shown. Teens may make an attempt to divide you, but you can overcome this by supporting each other consistently. Your young people will soon understand that living according to God's way is the best and makes for strong relationships. They will learn that you support them like you support each other, and will eventually come to appreciate this. They will learn that true love mandates rules and guidelines. Freedom of choice does not come about without responsibility. As they learn to accept this – and they will – they will develop a gauge to determine what life style will truly benefit them in the long run.

Pray for your children and demonstrate to them that their relationship with your new spouse will not take the place of their relationship with their other parent. That relationship will continue and, hopefully and prayerfully, will also grow. The new parent needs to be given a chance for a unique and different relationship, and demonstrating unity between you will help the children make the transition. A loving spouse can and will be a tremendous support in the healing process.

Be Faithful

It is extremely important to be faithful in your financial responsibility to your children who live elsewhere. There should be no pressure about this as both of you were aware of this obligation before you married. I would encourage ladies to support your husbands in this regard, and men to be faithful and responsible to your children. Be sure to put their interests ahead of yours. For example, they need your time. Instead of indulging in a hobby or going on vacation, invite them in on activities they can share with you. If you are going someplace they can go, call them and make arrangements to pick them up. Then be faithful. If an occasion arises when you can't pick them up, give them the courtesy of an explanation, but don't make broken promises a habit. Your children have had enough hurt and rejection already. In order to parent with integrity, you must put their needs and their welfare first. God will give you the means to meet your financial obligations, and equip you to do this cheerfully. As you do, you will become a tool in the healing process of your children. Your faithfulness will help maintain consistency and stability in their lives and prevent further blaming of themselves for the break-up of the family, which is very common among children of divorced parents.

In addition to being faithful to dates and visits, show genuine concern and interest in your children's activities, their likes and dislikes. When they're with you, don't drop them off and expect other people to watch them. Spend as much time with them as possible, not just quantity or even quality time, but determine it's going to be Godly time. Get them involved in good activities with Godly people who can speak life into them. When they are not with you, make it a priority to be at school events, open houses with teachers, sporting events or plays as often as possible. You may feel that the other parent sees to church-related activity or perhaps doesn't want them involved in church. However, when your children are with you, choose wisely. Your time is limited.

Being Involved Says "I Love You"

The following is applicable to all children but is mentioned here to point up the critical need in the lives of your children who live elsewhere. A recent report from the Department of Education stated that when a father is involved in the process, children do better in school.* The involvement is not in the form of doing homework with them every night, but rather in attending extra-curricular activities such as sporting events, plays, musicals, science fairs, etc. The children of involved fathers not only got better grades, but also were less likely to fail a grade, be suspended or expelled. Attendance at parent/teacher conferences is important too, according to the report. If you don't live with your children, the school will be understanding and set up extra conferences for you, Dad, to make sure you are involved at that level. This in no way minimizes the importance of the mother's involvement, but the report stated that a recent presidential memorandum urged all departments to include fathers in their policies and programs when possible. Education is one area where fathers can be most effective. This is true for single dads as well as those who are in a two-parent household. If you have a two-parent household, don't give the excuse that you are the major breadwinner and too busy to make school functions. You can do the things that will make a critical difference. Again, make it to extra-curricular activities and special conferences. Involvement with the children is important by phone, too, to make sure they are on the right course with school.

The following are guidelines for all parents, not just those with visiting children. Establish a regular time for your child to study. Create the right environment for learning. Talk with your children on a regular basis about their school day. Again, get involved with the school, and most importantly, set a good example. Reading is critical. If your children see you read, they will read also. This is an excellent place to mention Bible reading with your children and in front of them. Acknowledge the good efforts they make and be aware that if they are doing poorly in a particular subject, they may not be lacking the ability but the right kind of help. Help them seek the type of aid they need. That might mean going back to basics in the subject matter and doing some review. It might mean a season of tutoring or some other extra effort. With that in mind, be the encourager. As you do this, your children will conquer the difficulty, have more confidence in themselves and even become an example to their peers.

An important way of being involved with your daughters is by taking them out on dates from a very early age. Make these special dress-up events. When you take them out, bring them a flower or little toy to demonstrate how a Godly man should value them and treat them. Your daughters will eventually choose men to marry based on what they have experienced with you. Treat them with respect and good manners and they will grow to expect that of other men.

If you have sons, take them with you whenever possible and teach them what it means to be a Godly man by your mannerisms, dress and life style, how you treat others and what you allow into your home. All these things over time will count toward their character. If you have been faithful and reliable, a person of integrity, they will learn to make decisions and handle life from your example.

It is also important to support their decisions as they mature. That does not mean giving them blanket approval, but if you have given them good guidance, you will have an open channel to share your insight on important matters and then let them choose between specified options. As they get old enough to consider attending college or buying a vehicle, for example, give them some clear options and help them see the benefits of each choice. By the time they are ready to get married, you can have an established pattern of communication, sharing insight, prayer, and then supporting their decisions. By doing so, you will maintain the privilege and responsibility of an active role in their lives and the lives of your grandchildren. Be faithful, be interested in them, and fulfill your financial responsibilities to them.

It should be mentioned, that if you, as a father, experience a time in your life when circumstances force you to decrease your financial support, you must be honest and forthright with your former spouse. Explain the situation and still make the best partial payment you can. However, if you have possessions you can sell, do so and use the funds to help meet your responsibility to your children.

But I Didn't Plan On This

There are many women today who marry men whose children do not live with them, but they are fully aware of the moral and financial obligations to those children, and they do not object. They recognize their husband's responsibility and embrace it. However, many of these women have failed to count the cost in regard to the possibility of changing circumstances, which could bring these children into their homes. We have ministered to couples who have had almost overnight changes in custody, for any number of unforeseen reasons, bringing full responsibility for raising children into their hands and homes. Often, the wife is ill-equipped for mothering this instant family, just as I was to become an instant father to three young boys. It's generally easier to establish loving relationships with younger children. If the children are older, it could take a different approach and time frame to develop close bonds. Older children are dealing with a lot of life issues. Now they are thrust into a new situation with new demands. You are going to be a parent who is partly responsible for care, activities and discipline, and the way you and your spouse handle this will determine the growth of these new relationships. Here are a few insights to help you through these adjustments.

Don't resent them being in your home. You were fully aware of the children, even though you did not expect them to live with you. Now you will have the opportunity and privilege of helping to shape their lives. You must look at this with the love of God in your heart, and with the mercy and insight He will give you for them. You may have to reorganize your work schedule, and it will probably interfere with some of what you want to do. There will definitely be an adjustment period, but remember, this is an investment in lives. God will equip you for the task. Have as much open communication as possible and make the necessary adjustments cheerfully. Don't expect instant close relationship. You must "learn" each other. If you have a new daughter, take her out shopping and to favorite activities getting to know her interests and personality. Schoolwork and hobbies are also very important. You may have young sons to get to know and the same rules apply. Schoolwork, sports or other favorite hobbies enjoyed together are great ways of "learning" each other and developing friendly communication. You must make it clear that you are not taking the other parent's place, but that your relationship is separate and will be unique and different. Share with the child that you will work and grow together and do your best to help each other over the rough spots. Many of your feelings I felt too, so I encourage you to give these relationships time. They don't develop overnight. Your husband will support you. You want these children to learn that they can count on you, so be content being who you are and let them get to know the real you.

A word to husbands is in order here. Remember the principle of agreement. You and your wife must choose a course of family discipline, and you must support her when she exercises this responsibility with the children. Also, do not belittle her or downgrade her decisions in any way. Be supportive of her and once the children see that you are in harmony, it will be easier for them to become integrated in this new system. Give definite boundaries and then back them up. During the adjustment period, the children may try your patience. You may feel you do not have the patience, the love or the wisdom to give. I understand that and I know there is grace for you in this area.

Getting involved in a local church is so important to help stabilize your new family. If you can't agree on what church to attend, attend the church of your husband's choice right now, even though it may be different from what you are accustomed to. Start by going with him as an expression of your unity as a couple. There may be another

146

church where you would like to attend a Bible study or women's group and perhaps they have more to offer the children too. As your husband sees the fruit of your support and your willingness to be loving and flexible, he will eventually be better able to reach agreement on this issue of where to fellowship.

Many times women in blended families wish to have a baby of their own but feel they can not because of the children they are raising. This may not be a correct assumption, although there may need to be a waiting season. If this applies to you, talk with your husband even though he may already be aware of your desire. Discuss with him the importance to you of having a baby and the fact that this does not have to bring division in the family. In fact, the contentment of bearing a child together can bring peace and joy to both of you that will benefit the other children also. Your goal can be accomplished and, in the meantime, don't resent the children you already have. Developing relationships with these children will bring peace and unity that you can not even imagine today. God wants your family to be whole. He also wants you to have your heart's desire. He wants your family to live with purpose and to fulfill your destiny, and He's there to heal you and give you the resources you need.

Remember:
1. Discipline without anger.
2. Be faithful to dates, visits and financial responsibilities
3. Be involved in your children's lives and interests.
4. Have one set of rules for everyone.
5. "Learn" each other and develop productive communication.
6. Be yourself.

CHAPTER TWELVE

GRANDPARENTING IN THE BLENDED FAMILY

It is God's will to support our children and help them establish loving relationships. Has your son or daughter decided to marry someone who has children? How do you respond to this – support? disapproval? Or are your feelings about a second marriage uncertain and foreign, never having dealt with divorce and remarriage in your family before? Now that this decision is made, how you act rather than react can greatly influence the success of this new blended family. I can understand your feelings of uncertainty. However, in choosing to grandparent a blended family, you have a great opportunity to be used in the healing process of all family members, especially the children. Accepting them, loving them, and spending time with them is so important to the many adjustments they will have to make in the first few years. With the wisdom you have as a mature person, you can rise above your uncertain feelings with the Lord's help and develop stable, caring relationships that will do much to help them recover from their hurts. We know it is God's will to accomplish this and as you get to know each other, the children can get to know their new parent better through you. The new parent also has an opportunity, in showing respect and love to his own parents and from time to time, taking loving counsel, to let the children see him or her in a role similar to their own. This is a model you want to keep before them as the family develops loving, respectful and open communication. They will learn to weigh your input as they grow into adulthood.

The Two-way Door

In our particular case, both Lee's father and mine were deceased when we married, but we did have our mothers who each loved and accepted our children, and we thank God for that. Our mothers invested time and love in our children, creating open doors of communication and rich, nurturing relationships. The kids called both moms "Grandma" and made no distinction between the relationships. We found each grandparent to be an excellent sounding board and counselor during the first few years of our marriage. The children were able to talk freely with their Grandmas during this period of adjustment and, needless to say, they became very close to both of them.

This is not a one-sided investment of love and affection either. As you get into your senior years, you will realize the value of having children around you with their honest and caring love. In our own case, my mother lived with us for many years and our children learned much from her. Besides her good old-fashioned values, she taught them to cook traditional Italian dishes and to make cookies. She took them shopping and out on spontaneous trips for ice cream, usually at bedtime. Besides all she did for them, the children gave her more value and purpose, and helped fill the gaps in her life as a widow. This was a two-way door always open to the flow of love, affection and acceptance. When my mother became debilitated with cancer, our children spent nights with her and cared for her physical needs at the end of her life. This was something they wanted to do, which also gave my siblings and me a brief respite. Our children were there when my mother went on to be with the Lord and they still talk about the experience today. They love to reminisce about her love, her care, her sense of humor and her travels. This investment of love is beneficial for all and worth more than can be measured.

I can say the same for my mother-in-law who, over the years, has also expressed the same love, concern and care for our children. She has never lived with us but our children chose to spend many nights with her, even as young adults, enjoying her company and providing her with quality companionship. There is still an enriching process going on as she sows into their lives from her perspective, and she enjoys their company as much today as ever.

Grandparents, try not to show favoritism to grandchildren of your other sons or daughters. Our mothers were wonderful in this way, never buying more valuable gifts for their "natural" grandchildren or playing favorites in other obvious ways. Thus, they helped knit the whole family together and helped create security for the ones with so many new facets of relationship developing.

"Whatsoever A Man Sows..."

We can speak first-hand about grandparenting since we have four grandchildren – two girls and two boys – from our oldest son and his wife. Remember that initially, their marriage was stormy, but their relationship has matured and grown over eleven years. They lived with us for a while and, in fact, I had the privilege of teaching my precious "daughter-in-love" to cook. I got to spend valuable time with her in those critical early years. I chose to love and care for them and to leave old issues alone. Things that were dealt with in the past were left in the past. With regard to my injury, the Lord used the births of my grandchildren, especially the first one, to bring about great healing in my life. I was able to show them love without the pain of separation that I experienced with my daughter.

However, there came a time when our son and daughter-in-law decided to move out of state. They had three children at that time and the fourth was born while they were away. This almost three year period when I could not see my grandchildren was very difficult as they had lived with us, and they filled a great void in my life at that time. I chose not to become resentful or bitter but to follow a higher road, submitting my feelings to the Lord. I recognized that through prayer and a loving relationship with them, someday they would move back to our area. I sent our grandchildren a box every month or so filled with Bible coloring books, crayons, construction paper or little things to do or to wear. I was not trying to buy their love, but I was letting them know that even though we lived eighteen hundred miles away, they were still very much a part of our lives. Phone calls are great, but for children, going to the post office to receive a box addressed to them was like finding treasure. They would open the boxes to find little toys, games, books – little inexpensive things really – but they made memories not easily forgotten. It's a joy to hear them talk about those times, sharing what they experienced opening "Papa boxes" from New York. How they looked forward to each one, and it gave them a sense of belonging to us back here.

I encourage grandparents to invest some time and some little inexpensive things in your grandchildren, and send them on a regular basis, even if they don't live far away. This will fill gaps when they are away from you and create special memories and a sense of belonging.

A couple of years ago, I built a small fort in the woods for our grandchildren which our first granddaughter named "Chapel Fort", and that's exactly what it is. I take the kids down there and we have church! We sing, pray and even have an offering which, at Christmas time, is sent to American Indian children, a charity chosen by the children themselves. What this does is teach them about day-to-day Christianity – living and giving. We pray together, sing together and the older ones read scriptures and share. They always look forward to going to the fort, and after "church", they play in the woods on their little mountain.

Only the Lord knows what this time will mean to them in adult life and in eternity. They are learning to give, to pray for one another and to enjoy the beautiful surroundings of God's creation.

I thank the Lord that I have recently been able to start exercising and working out regularly for the first time since the injury, and I purchased some exercise equipment. I take our grandchildren with me when I exercise and they not only watch me and talk as I work out, but I've set up a little program for each of them, ages five, six, eight and ten. It's amazing how this has helped build up their self-confidence. This is not a weight-lifting program, but time spent with me when they can use the equipment under my supervision. They learn about working together and about having a healthy body, soul and mind. Lee adds other aspects of love and tenderness to grandparenting, and it's wonderful how we balance each other out in our relationships with the children. They each bring such a wonderful dimension to our family, and each of us is able to contribute something different to their growth and development. It's not only a joy to interact with our grandchildren, but it's a privilege to help our son and daughter-in-law sow destiny and purpose into their children's lives.

Aunts and uncles in the blended family can respond in the same way as grandparents. Choosing to show love and acceptance has far-reaching effects. Most of our brothers and sisters accepted our family and spent time with all of our children as we did with theirs. However, we also had a sibling who had difficulty accepting the blended family. Our response was still one of love and compassion. There will be less than best situations, but you can keep praying, believing and working for change. Do not allow other people's choices to control your life or your new family. Your attitude will make the difference, and everywhere you find a relative open to these loving, nurturing relationships, cultivate them. They are priceless.

Do It Now!

You might be a grandparent whose grandchildren are in a situation that does not permit you to spend time with them. I still encourage you to invest whatever time you can through cards, notes or small gifts. Make a phone call to your grandchild's parent explaining that you understand the differences the couple has had, and that you still want to be an active, loving and supportive grandparent. You may get a more favorable response than you think. These are difficult situations and it might take time to develop this type of communication, but be persistent. Be loving, understanding, caring and always praying for the relationship you desire with your grandchildren to develop.

As you are waiting for this, don't allow the void in your life to keep you from being an active part of other children's lives. There are children next door, around the block or at church who may not have a grandparent or even a loving parent. Use this opportunity out of your own void to be involved with other children through church, a big brother or sister program, or just find a neighborhood kid who needs someone. Begin to pour love and your years of experience and maturity into young people. You will find great joy and contentment sowing these seeds, and someday you may be able to spend this kind of time with your own grandchildren. Continue to be faithful to these children whom you have chosen to love and befriend, even when relationships with your grandchildren open up. Only in eternity will the rewards be made fully known for the time and love you have invested.

Remember:
1. All children need love and acceptance.

2. Love is a two-way door.
3. Don't play favorites.
4. Seeds sown will bring a harvest.
5. Share what you can TODAY.

CHAPTER THIRTEEN

THE SIGNIFICANCE OF THE LOCAL CHURCH

It is the will of God that we are active members of a local church, a functioning member of a body of believers. The local church has enormous significance, not only to the blended family but to our nation as a whole. If the church truly teaches and demonstrates that once we have come to the Lord, "our sins are as far as the east is from the west", it can have a tremendous impact on the process of healing (Psalm 103:12). The body of Christ should demonstrate that our past does not have to handicap us the rest of our lives and that indeed, divorce is not the unpardonable sin. With over half of first-time marriages ending in divorce, the local church and its leadership must take the forefront in this battle for the family, both in terms of prevention and healing.

Every family needs the teaching of the Word, the demonstration of the love of Christ, acceptance and the opportunity to serve the Lord without prejudice. My first experience with a local church was right after my conversion when the man who led me to the Lord invited me to a service. I accepted his invitation with reluctance, due to the fact that after people divorce, the attitudes of friends, family and co-workers tend to change somewhat toward them. However, I was pleasantly surprised to find that the pastor, the leadership and the people of the church accepted my daughter and me and loved us. This was the beginning of my road to recovery from the pain of divorce. My pastor was a gifted teacher and he invited me to his home for dinner. He took the opportunity to invest in me as an individual. Other families also followed his example, inviting me to their homes and getting to know me. Their acceptance was welcomed. If they had questions, I answered them honestly. However, they did not pry into my past. Their Christ-like love was important in my life and my daughter's. This is the local church where I would meet my lovely wife and her three sons who would eventually become our sons. This church's investment in me was immeasurable and eternal as they planted the seeds of healing.

As a single police officer, my social activities began to change as I yielded my life more and more. I began to learn Bible principles and started on a new course. There were two men in particular in this church who took me under their wings, so to speak, and began to disciple me. The man who led me to salvation was one and the other was a professional firefighter who, like me, understood the dangers and stresses of a life of public service. With his age and maturity in God, he gave me great wisdom and insight, especially with regard to my employment. He cautioned me, for instance, not to always share my spiritual experiences at work, but to let my new life of faith speak for itself. The men at work would need to see changes in my attitudes, in the way I handled situations, and what I did with my time when I was not at work. This acceptance by the church family was a critical part of my ability to develop new life patterns.

It was almost four years later that Lee and I married. We then attended a much larger church that offered all aspects of family fellowship: Sunday school, children's church, youth group activities and more. The Lord called me into ministry and it was here, because of the graciousness of the pastor, I was allowed to attend Bible school, which I paid for by cooking staff breakfasts. Our sons became members of the youth group, church band and other activities. They had a youth pastor with whom they could sit and talk openly, and this was a great benefit to the family. My wife taught Sunday school and we all grew and changed in this loving environment. After serving this church for over four years, we decided to send our children to a Christian school which had recently opened in our area, so we began to attend the church that was providing Christian education. However, we found attitudes in this church to be different from those in the two previous churches we had attended and served. We found a legalistic and judgmental attitude toward divorced and remarried people. We did not let this discourage us and, in fact, we became members of this church. I offered my services to the pastors there in any way I could serve, whether cooking a meal for someone who was sick, cleaning the church, helping to set up school, etc. Eventually, the pastors began inviting me on home and hospital visits. As the years progressed, the attitudes of these men changed and in time, I became a deacon, an elder, then a trustee, and eventually a staff pastor at this church. Lee and I had a burden for families. With the senior pastor's approval, I began a monthly men's ministry, teaching and helping to equip men as heads of their homes, and vital members of the community. Out of this ministry, other churches began inviting me to come and share with their men.

Our three sons graduated from the Christian school receiving such distinguished awards as Student of the Year, Athlete of the Year, and other character and achievement merits. Our daughter also received awards from the school and my wife served as a primary teacher there for approximately four years. Our entire family received from this church, but we were also able to give something back. As we determined to overcome obstacles and attitudes to serve the Lord, our gifts made room for us (Proverbs 18:16). Along with tithes and offerings, we demonstrated that a blended family can bring strength and encouragement to others going through difficult times. At this church, we ministered and taught principles of marriage and family. We encouraged others to learn from the past and to be open to healing. By yielding and submitting ourselves to the

Lord and to the leadership of a local church, we can implant the wisdom we have learned into others so they don't have to travel the same road. This is a reciprocal relationship. As the church strengthens the family, the family can give back to the church in many different ways.

Let's examine the prejudice that is still in many churches across our nation. In the last few years the church, as a whole, has begun dealing with prejudice among cultures and denominations. However, there is still a great prejudice against divorced and remarried people and single parents. I'm not throwing stones at church leadership, but just giving counsel to readers in ministry. Prejudice simply means prejudging, which we should not do to anyone because of his culture, background or even because he or she is divorced and remarried. By getting to know each family individually, you will be better able to minister to each one, and also to receive ministry from them. Blended families are looking for the local church to be loving, accepting, forgiving and faithful. After all, isn't this what the church is supposed to offer to all? Keep in mind that it is through the blood of Christ that we all find acceptance and salvation. Often times, people say we serve a God of second chances. In reality, we serve a God of many chances. How many times have we all failed and fallen on our faces, so to speak, and needed His forgiveness and renewing power again? As long as we walk with a humble spirit and forgiveness toward one another, we can be used by the Lord as instruments of healing for hurting individuals and families.

The local church, unfortunately, is experiencing the same kind of "splitting up" that many Christian families are encountering. You might ask yourself why I would discuss church splits in a book about blended families. The reason is because a church split is a divorce. It is sad that many fine pastors and church leaders are subjected to gossip and events that eventually lead to the church splitting. What does a church split do to the church family? It separates loved ones and tears at deeply forged bonds, wreaking havoc in the lives and emotions of all involved, just as a divorce does to an individual family.

An area of ministry I have been involved in over the years is helping local church boards to resolve conflict trying to prevent church splits. Overcoming a church split after the fact is much like overcoming a divorce. We must not, in trying to resolve problems, be involved in the blame game and the pointing of fingers. There is enough responsibility to go around. However, repentance – asking God's forgiveness and each other's forgiveness – is the start of healing for all. Many people in the church split are like some divorced people. They never get over it. They continually replay in their minds the hurts, the pains and the questions. I understand the questions. I encourage pastors to work with their boards, to have as much communication as possible and to work out difficulties with a Christ-like attitude. You may achieve the desired goal with the wrong attitude and discover that no one has been the winner. If you have already experienced a church split, don't allow it to hinder your future ministry. God is used to beginning with nothing.

Church leaders should give blended families, and indeed all families, faithfulness, perseverance and the example of compassion that is so desperately needed. If you are a church leader, examine yourself as I have examined myself through divorce. Be willing to change. Be willing to submit yourself to the Lord in this area and He will give you greater wisdom, insight and understanding for your flock. You will be a stronger man or woman of God, a stronger family leader and a stronger shepherd.

My advice to all people is to support your pastor with prayer, tithing and service. Do not gossip, but send cards and notes of encouragement to your pastor and be available to help. These men and women are on the front lines of battle for our welfare.

I like to make the correlation of the local church with a fort in the days when our nation was young and moving westward. The fort provided families with security from enemies, needed supplies, a place of worship and a school room for their children. Our educational system until the early 1900's was the churches, and we had a better system when the church took its responsibility to not only preach the gospel, but also to live and demonstrate the Word of God. The fort was also a haven for families. When the fort bell rang, families knew there was an approaching enemy and they would soon be under attack. They would gather together in the security of the fort. I believe every church bell in America must ring today. The Christian churches and families of our nation are under attack by many forces. Secular media and entertainment, some political circles and liberal theology are just a few examples. Men and women of God, pastors, leadership, we must STAY IN THE FIGHT! Much is at stake. Build your local church as a fort and be a loving, caring stronghold to all who are dealing with the assaults of modern life. Remember, no weapon formed against you will ever prosper. Walk in love, walk in power, walk in forgiveness.

Called Alongside To Help

There are also other ministries that we should consider being a part of that will encourage and teach us, and be used by God to help bring us to wholeness. Many of these ministries also proclaim the Word of God to those who have yet to hear. Christian television and radio are among these ministries. As a nation, we are privileged and fortunate to have men and women, both past and present, who are willing to pay the price to provide full-time Christian communications media. Television and radio are valuable assets to us in that no matter where we go, we can have prayer support, inspirational music and teaching day or night. We can also become a part of getting the message to others who have not heard of the grace of God. I could tell much about how inspirational music played a great part in my healing, but let me just encourage you to allow Christian media to play a role in your life, and to involve yourself at some level for the benefit of others. The programming is diversified and some of it may not be your cup of tea, but look beyond that remembering that the body of Christ is diverse. Christian stations provide a variety of ministries to reach many different needs and tastes, but be wise and permit them to come into your home. There are many quality programs for children, teens and young adults, and the gospel is being preached to those who are without Christ.

Many nights, due to my injury, I was unable to sleep and could not do much reading either. TCT, our Christian network, coupled with my service at the local church, was a great encouragement and allowed me to grow in the things of God. Hearing the Word, praise and worship in the wee hours of the night strengthened me through the dark seasons of depression. Many men and women, preaching and teaching, helped bring wholeness to me by encouraging the changes that continually needed to be made. In all of our lives, Christian media can be an integral part of becoming the man or woman, the spouse or parent that each of us is called to become. I encourage you not only to be an active member of your local church, but also to give alms to outside ministries to enable the message to reach others. I shared how the Lord used this when our daughter ran away. We see the will of God accomplished when we are active members of a local body and when we support other ministries that are doing work outside the church walls. Let's pray for one another, let's believe for one another and let's reach out to a lost and hurting world.

Remember:
1. Be an active member of a local church.
2. Be supportive with your prayers, your service and your finances.
3. Be open to teaching.
4. Your gift will make room for you.
5. Be involved in and supportive of outside ministries.

CHAPTER FOURTEEN

REFLECTIONS FROM OUR ADULT CHILDREN

In preparing this book, we asked our four children if they had any thoughts on being raised in a blended family that they would like to share with our readers, and they all responded positively. We hope you find some insights in their reflections.

"In building a new family, we gain from each other to strengthen the whole. We become dependent upon each other for support and encouragement. When we put aside our differences for the greater good of the family, we begin to grow as a unit and individually as well. I believe that we only prosper when each individual puts down his or her feelings of resentment or bitterness and begins to work together. The key word is "work" until the cooperation becomes second nature, and love and acceptance must be the motivating force.

In the delicate matter of parenting a blended family, the feelings of children should not be overlooked. They, too, have been through the trauma of divorce. They are not only hurt but confused. Often, their thoughts and fears are ignored while adults are sorting out issues and emotions, seeking some sort of peaceful resolution. Encourage your child/children to express their feelings and BE SURE they know they are not responsible for the break-up of the family. Do not let your children live with questions in their hearts. Our children are our most precious gift. We must give them the love and protection they need, especially in the endeavor to start a new family. I suppose it is like building a new city where one once stood. First, you must deal with the rubble and ruins that remain from the former. Then you must lay a proper foundation in order for the new to succeed. This takes time. It may seem, at first, that you are just existing together, but if you are faithful, you will see your efforts bear fruit.

If you are a teen-ager having to adjust to a new family since Mom or Dad has remarried, remember these few things. Your parents love you, they want the best for you, and they are trying to give you a home where you have the influence of two parents. They are attempting to rebuild their lives in relationship with another person, and to give you the future you deserve. We only grow up to be strong human beings when we look into the face of adversity and decide to make the best of what we have, and strive to be the best person we can be regardless of the circumstances of our past. We also must remember that the past IS the past. We must take from it what we can learn and apply it to the future so as not to make the same mistakes we have witnessed. If you do not make the choice to leave the past behind, you are doomed to repeat it.

I know the hurts and feelings that many of you experience. I had the same questions and spent much time searching myself for the answers. It was not until I was grown that I realized that the answers were in giving up the resentment I held for the parents that God gave me. My mother and new father married when I was about eleven years old. They tried everything to have a happy home, but I was never satisfied. I harbored many wrong feelings toward anyone who tried to make me feel loved. The problems with my childhood rested with me. I refused to give up my bitterness and to let my new father be just that – my father. I missed out on a lot of happy times because I chose to be miserable. I thank God every day for my father's persistence. He chose to love me even when that love was not reciprocated. It was because of that love that I have seen the error of my ways. When I look back now, I realize that I wasted so many years that could have been spent learning more from him. He stepped up to the plate for me so many times as he saw the pain and struggle I endured. He is the one I go to when frustration is too much to handle.

It was only when I learned that the problems with our relationship were there because I held resentment in my heart and was allowing bitterness to rule my life, that I was able to ask forgiveness and begin to build a secure relationship with the man who had always been, and always would be, my Dad. You see, when we don't care about the feelings of the others in our families, we can not grow to our full potential and the entire family suffers. The rebuilding is like a long, and sometimes tiring journey, but the rewards are worth all the effort."

Joe

"I don't think I really had much of a problem with living in a blended family. I was very young when my Dad remarried. I was excited though. I liked my new Mom and brothers a lot. I never thought of them as taking the place of my natural mother, but rather I thought of them as an addition to what I already had. I thought of myself as now having three grandmas instead of two. Who would pass up another grandma? If one looks at the situation as an addition and not a replacement, it makes life a lot easier. The way I looked at it was that there was plenty of love to go around so the more the merrier! A new Mom to cook and welcome me home from school and three new brothers to play with – I didn't have a problem with that. It wasn't difficult for me because I didn't really remember my natural parents together. Even though we weren't biologically related, my new Mom and I looked so much like each other that people couldn't believe we were related only through marriage! I think the biggest thing is how you look at it. Addition should be stressed over replacement.

The Lord may have to help you deal with it, but all you have to do is ask Him."

Jennifer

"Being raised in a blended family was a real learning experience for me. I was very young when my father left and I don't remember very much about him being in our home. Therefore, there were about eight years of my life when I didn't know what it was like to have a father in our home. It was just the four of us – Mom, my two brothers and myself. It seemed like it was always going to be just the four of us. We each had our own opinions and feelings about what was going to happen when Mom and John began to date. I was probably the most different of the three of us in that I had the least amount of bitterness and resentment toward my Dad for events that occurred in our lives. So when we knew that Mom and John were going to get married, I didn't take it as something that was going to break up or change what we had. I knew for myself that what I really wanted was to have a father who was going to be there for us and do things with us. I wanted someone I could trust when he said, 'I'm going to do this or that'. I wanted to know it would really happen and not always have to wait and see.

I remember a lot of times before they were married doing things with John – going to Grandma's house, playing catch or just gathering up our cousins and going on a picnic. Those are the things that meant the most to me because we were a complete family. After they married, we continued to do a lot of things together – not only small things but we learned how to work together. We put all our efforts together and ran a small business, for example. We learned a work ethic, how to help each other and how to help others. More importantly, we learned more about the

Bible and about life. I guess what I'm trying to say is that when Mom and John married, I finally had a father who was always there for me. I didn't lose a relationship with my biological father and I wasn't as hurt by some of the events in that relationship because I knew that at home, we would always be together and do things together.

We went through some changes by moving, going through junior and senior high school and changing schools. Sometimes I didn't agree with a decision that was made or I had my own opinion about it, but all in all, when a decision was made, I trusted it was going to bring about good results and it always did. I trusted that Mom and John always wanted what was best for us and knew what was best for us, despite the fact that I might have wanted to do something else. I was able to accept their decisions, knowing that they knew better than we did what was good for us. I think that all we went through together, good times or bad, drew us closer together because we were able to communicate with each other.

I think the key for a child is his or her attitude toward the new parent. The fact that Mom and John dated for almost four years really helped us to get to know him. He wasn't someone totally new when he came into our household. Also, I was able to see things a little differently – like how Mom worked so hard and seemed to always be doing whatever it took to provide for us. I saw almost a need for a husband and definitely for me and my brothers, the need for a father in our home.

If I were to talk to a couple who was planning to be married and one or both of them had children, I would have to tell them to really get to know the other children, and be able to communicate effectively with them before marriage. I think they should discuss with the children the reasons why they are getting married and talk about their need for each other. Once married, they should include the children in discussions and treat each child as an individual with specific needs of his or her own. They must be able to listen to the children when they talk, and encourage them to express their feelings and ideas. The new family needs to spend as much time together as possible, whether reading or playing games at the kitchen table like we used to do, so the children feel welcome in your space and time. They should feel nothing is holding them back if they want to come to you with a need or a problem.

To a young person who has a parent who is remarrying I would say to trust that your Mom or Dad is making the right decision for themselves and that they have your best interest in mind. Don't just think of yourself, but think of the needs of your parents as well. Never feel that your parent is getting married and is going to exclude you or let someone else take your place. I would also say to give the new parent a chance, and to try to communicate with that person as much as possible and learn about him or her. You, too, can develop a new relationship characterized by mutual love and respect, open communication and real trust if you are willing to do your part."

Jason

The following is an excerpt from a personal letter written to me in 1996 and reprinted here with permission:

"Dear John,

...I was talking to Grace (not her real name) last week and she was telling me how her boys, when they were younger, all went through a rebellious period. She continued by saying that her husband was an alcoholic back then and was not much help to her if any at all. He has since become a born-again Christian, thank God. I guess what I'm getting at is that as we talked, it made me think back to when I was younger. I recall staying up all night begging Mom not to get married again. Now I am beginning to see how selfish and immature I was, only thinking of myself and not Mom. Working with Grace has been uplifting and a real blessing to me...As I talked to her that day, it seemed as if she were telling me about myself, only with a different point of view than I ever had before. I began to think of how Mom always worked, shopped and cooked for us and yet, always had time to throw the football with us or go out and buy us a baseball glove. She even taught us how to pitch and catch when we played baseball. I never thought that maybe she needed someone, that she may have needed help and support that we kids couldn't give her.

John, I realize that I was never an easy child to understand. I never made things simple. It was my way of being rebellious, I guess, not necessarily to anyone in particular, just to be rebellious. I may never have told you how much I appreciate you and that I'm thankful for the Father you have been to me since I was a boy until this very day and for many more years to come. I also pray for your forgiveness for my attitude in my rebellious years and that we could continue to grow closer. I do appreciate all the things you've been to me in my life: a father, a teacher, a friend, a provider, a helper, a counselor, a supporter and so much more.

I thank God that I learned how to work hard and to be persistent and responsible, which are all things that I may never have known without you and without Mom's decision to ignore my plea and marry again.

People tell me all the time what a respectful person I am and that I am a joy to work with, and someone always says 'Boy, your parents did a good job with you'. You know what? I'm not patting myself on the back at all, because that statement is true. Someone did a very good job – you and Mom. I only do things and act the way I learned to be at home. It just took me this long to realize it...I hope you understand what I've said today, and it was nice to be able to share some things with you that I've learned over time... Talk to you soon...

Jim

FINAL THOUGHTS

As we have seen, the family faces many challenges and obstacles that could, if not worked through, put us on a road to destruction from generation to generation. However, we have also seen a piece of God's blueprint in each of these chapters. If we yield ourselves to these truths, we will not only strengthen ourselves, but also provide the atmosphere and attitude for our spouses and children to be changed and healed. Yielding to the Word of God enables us to meet the challenges and make changes, and encourages our loved ones by demonstrating that it CAN be done. The mercy and truth of the living God gives us purpose, productivity and the ability to recognize that no matter where we have been, our future is going to be very different. All couples go through seasons of trial. However, as we learn the principles of faithfulness, commitment and longevity, we will be strengthened. You will also have seasons when all things are going well. Enjoy these, but don't leave your prayer life and the foundations you've learned through your struggles.

I liken it to combat training for a police officer. I trained and worked out with weights in all seasons of my life. Then when the storms came, I was prepared. As we prepare ourselves physically, mentally, emotionally and spiritually, we will be better able to handle difficulties and will not be thrown off course. We may stumble at times and have seasons of tears, but we will not be dealt a death blow.

As parents, is there a particular age, marital status or season of life when you stop praying for your children? The answer is simply "No!" And remember, we are not going to allow our children's decisions to handicap us in life. If poor decisions are made, we have learned that we must not react, but rather act out of principle – with prayer, thanksgiving, and speaking blessing over our children, not negativity. Be faithful to God's ways and continue in prayer, and He will make the blueprint for your family very specific.

Single parents, you do not have to be married to produce a wholesome family life for your children. As you allow the Lord to become more real to you in your daily life, your hurts will be healed, and joy and contentment will pervade your character. He will give you a greater confidence in who you are in God and will help you produce a solid home life for your family. Take some pressure off yourself by becoming the Mom or Dad that you can be, realizing that you can not be both parents. The other aspect of parenting can be provided by a loving local church, where men and women of character can invest time in your children. As your children see the changes in you and the love of their church environment, they will begin to overcome their issues, grow and become productive. There may come a time when you will meet a prospective spouse. It is important that you develop this relationship based on real love and Godly character so that this person will commit to you and your family, embracing the children's needs.

The same applies to readers who have never been married. Single people can also have a wholesome, happy life. Take the time necessary to mature in God and become the person you want to be, and He will direct your steps.

Following are several blank pages. This is your chapter. It is not the last chapter, for I believe that for many, this could be a new beginning. God is looking for people who are willing to be made whole (John 5:6) and then go out and give a cup of cold water in His name. These pages are for you to fill in with great hope and promise, recognizing that God loves you. Accept and receive that. Don't meditate on the past, but start where you are right now. Develop a spirit of thanks, praise, prayer and contentment. It takes time, but through your trials and tribulations, you will gain strength and wisdom. Speak to your spouse and your children, not as circumstances or emotions would dictate, but as God speaks into your heart. Look at them as God looks at you. He has your best in mind and He sees you whole. He wants to empower you to grow and prosper. May the Lord grant you wisdom, strength, peace and the motivation to follow His blueprint each and every day. The next chapter is yours to write.

APPENDIX

Net Worth Worksheet #1

<u>ASSETS</u>
1. Cash
   On hand $____
   Checking   ____
   Savings   ____
   Total cash $_____
2. $ loaned to others   _____
3. Investments
   Savings bonds   ____
   Stocks & bonds   ____
   Mutual funds   ____
   Life Ins cash value   ____
   Annuity Cash value   ____
   Total Investments   _____
4. Real Estate (Market Value)
   Home   ____
   Other   ____
   Other   ____
   Total Real Estate   _____
5. Other Property (Market Value)
   Cars   ____
   Boat, camper, etc.   ____
   Small business   ____
   Furniture   ____
   Collectibles   ____
   Personal (jewelry, etc.)   ____
   Other   ____
   Total   _____

6. TOTAL ASSETS $_____

Net Worth Worksheet #2

<u>LIABILITIES</u>

7. Unpaid current bills
    Taxes $____
    Utilities   ____
    Other   ____
    Total Unpaid Bills $_____
8. Installment Loans (Bal. Due)
    Car   ____
    Charge Accts.   ____
    Credit Cards   ____
    Total Installment Loans   _____
9. Loans (Bal. Due)
    Bank   ____
    School   ____
    Other   ____
    Total Loans Due   _____
10. Mortgage loans (Bal. Due)
    Home   ____
    Real Estate   ____
    Other   ____
    Total Mortgage Loans   _____

11. Total Liabilities $_____

                    Total Assets (6) $_____
                        Minus
                    Total Liabilities $_____

                    Net Worth $_____

                    Date_____

SPENDABLE INCOME WORKSHEET

Date_____

DEDUCTIONS FROM PAY	HUSBAND	WIFE
Federal Income Tax	$_____	$_____
State Income Tax	_____	_____
Social security	_____	_____
Pension	_____	_____
Hospitalization	_____	_____
Life Insurance	_____	_____
Savings Bonds	_____	_____
Credit Union savings	_____	_____
Credit Union payments	_____	_____
Stock options	_____	_____
Union dues	_____	_____
Christmas club	_____	_____
Other	_____	_____
TOTAL DEDUCTIONS	_____	_____
TOTAL PAY	_____	_____
MINUS TOTAL DEDUCTIONS	_____	_____
TAKE HOME PAY	_____	_____

INCOME COMPILATION

Take Home Pay	$_____
Other Income	
Rentals	_____
Interest & Dividends	_____
Royalties	_____
Business	_____
Other	_____
TOTAL SPENDABLE INCOME	$_____

DEBT WORKSHEET

OWED TO	BAL. DUE	INTEREST	MINIMUM MONTHLY

MONTHLY INCOME & EXPENSES #1

Income per month

Salary	$_____
Interest	_____
Dividends	_____
Notes	_____
Rents	_____
Total Gross Income	$_____

LESS
1. Tithe _____
2. Tax _____
Net Spendable Income _____

3. Housing _____
   Mort/rent _____
   Ins. _____
   Taxes _____
   Electric _____
   Gas _____
   Water _____
   Sanitation _____
   Phone _____
   Maint. _____
   Other _____
4. Food _____
5. Auto _____
   Payments _____
   Gas/Oil _____
   Insurance _____
   License _____
   Taxes _____
   Maint/Repair _____
   Dep. @.08/mi _____

MONTHLY INCOME & EXPENSES #2

6. Insurance   _____
   - Life   _____
   - Medical   _____
   - Other   _____
7. Debts   _____
   - Credit card   _____
   - Loans/notes   _____
   - Other   _____
8. Enter/Recreation   _____
   - Eating out   _____
   - Trips   _____
   - Babysitters   _____
   - Activities   _____
   - Vacation   _____
   - Other   _____
9. Clothing   _____
   ($10/mo/person)
10. Savings   _____
11. Medical Expenses   _____
    - Doctor   _____
    - Dentist   _____
    - Medications   _____
    - Other   _____
12. Miscellaneous   _____
    - Toiletries/cosmetics   _____
    - Beauty/Barber   _____
    - Laundry/cleaning   _____
    - Lunches/allowances   _____
    - Books/magazines   _____
    - Gifts   _____
    - Special Education   _____
    - Investments   _____
    - Other   _____
    - TOTAL EXPENSES $_____

MONTHLY INCOME & EXPENSES #3

INCOME VS. EXPENSES

Net Spendable Income (from page 1) $_____

Less Total Expenses (from page 2)   _____

                                                          $ _____

INCOME APPLICATION:

   Cash $_____

   Checking _____

   Savings   _____

WORKS CITED

Holy Bible, all references are from the King James Version unless otherwise noted.

*Ashcraft, Michael, "Dads Can Make a Big Difference In School Success." <u>Western New York Family</u> May 1998: 42.

ABOUT THE AUTHORS

John Guadagno is a veteran police officer who survived exposure to toxic chemicals in 1981 while on duty at a train derailment. He has overcome tremendous injury and has been in ministry for over twenty years. Lee is a registered nurse pursuing a Master's degree in Natural Health. They have four children and four grandchildren who all reside in Western New York.

John and Lee are ordained ministers and founders of God's Blueprint Ministries. They have been involved in a variety of work over the years including staff pastor, prison ministry, marriage and family seminars and conferences. Because of his unique background in law enforcement and ministry, John believes that his call is to establish men and women in God's Word and to offer tools and resources to facilitate healing of individuals and families. Together, they have developed a teaching style that is frank, genuine and warm. John and Lee have created a unique tape series called "Walking Through Legal Entanglements" which addresses the practical and spiritual sides of domestic/family issues, personal injury/compensation issues and other court-related situations you may find yourself in. (See back page for ordering information.) They are convinced that because of God's overwhelming love, He will never leave us or forsake us.

John and Lee are available for limited ministry engagements.

We hope this book has been an encouragement and a help to you and your family. If you have realized your need of Jesus Christ through reading this book, we urge you to commit your life and your future to His Lordship. You may pray along these lines.

Heavenly Father,

I recognize my need of Jesus, so I turn from my own ways and submit myself to You. I believe Jesus died on the cross for my sins and I receive your forgiveness and a new beginning. I ask you to change my heart and mind and help me to become the person you have destined me to be. Please fill me with the Holy Spirit and have Your way in my life. Thank you for taking me as I am. I determine to know you and serve you for the rest of my life. I give thanks in the name of Your Son, Jesus. Amen.

If you have sincerely prayed that prayer or if this book has had an impact on your life, please contact us so we can rejoice with you. You may write us at

Sword of the Spirit Ministries

300 Kensington Avenue

Buffalo, New York 14214

Assoc. Pastor John A. Guadagno

hope4u@localnet.com

ook

Other books you will enjoy reading

APOSTLES, PROPHETS AND THE COMING MOVES OF GOD
by Dr. Bill Hamon.
Author of the "Prophets" series, Dr. Bill Hamon brings the same anointed instruction in this new series on apostles! Learn about the apostolic age and how apostles and prophets work together. Find out God's end-time plans for the Church!
ISBN 0-939868-09-1

PROPHETS AND PERSONAL PROPHECY
by Dr. Bill Hamon.
This book defines the role of a prophet or prophetess and gives the reader strategic guidelines for judging prophecy. Many of the stories included are taken from Dr. Bill's ministry and add that "hands on" practicality that is quickly making this book a best-seller.
ISBN 0-939868-03-2

PROPHETS AND THE PROPHETIC MOVEMENT
by Dr. Bill Hamon.
This sequel to *Prophets and Personal Prophecy* is packed with the same kind of cutting instruction that made the first volume a best-seller. Prophetic insights, how-to's, and warnings make this book essential for the Spirit-filled church.
ISBN 0-939868-04-0

PROPHETS, PITFALLS, AND PRINCIPLES
by Dr. Bill Hamon.
This book shows you how to recognize your hidden "root" problems, and detect and correct character flaws and "weed seed" attitudes. It also can teach you how to discern true prophets using Dr. Hamon's ten M's.
ISBN 0-939868-05-9

Other books you will enjoy reading

NO MORE SOUR GRAPES

by Don Nori.

Who among us wants our children to be free from the struggles we have had to bear? Who among us wants the lives of our children to be full of victory and love for their Lord? Who among us wants the hard-earned lessons from our lives given freely to our children? All these are not only possible, they are also God's will. You can be one of those who share the excitement and joy of seeing your children step into the destiny God has for them. If you answered "yes" to these questions, the pages of this book are full of hope and help for you and others just like you.

ISBN 0-7684-2037-7

THE POWER OF BROKENNESS

by Don Nori.

Accepting Brokenness is a must for becoming a true vessel of the Lord, and is a stepping-stone to revival in our hearts, our homes, and our churches. Brokenness alone brings us to the wonderful revelation of how deep and great our Lord's mercy really is. Join this companion who leads us through the darkest of nights. Discover the *Power of Brokenness*.

ISBN 1-56043-178-4

SECRETS OF THE MOST HOLY PLACE

by Don Nori.

Here is a prophetic parable you will read again and again. The winds of God are blowing, drawing you to His Life within the Veil of the Most Holy Place. There you begin to see as you experience a depth of relationship your heart has yearned for. This book is a living, dynamic experience with God!

ISBN 1-56043-076-1

IN PURSUIT OF PURPOSE

Best-selling author Myles Munroe reveals here the key to personal fulfillment: purpose. We must pursue purpose because our fulfillment in life depends upon our becoming what we were born to be and do. *In Pursuit of Purpose* will guide you on that path to finding purpose.

ISBN 1-56043-103-2

Other books you will enjoy reading

THE GOD CHASERS (Best-selling **Destiny Image** book)
by Tommy Tenney.
There are those so hungry, so desperate for His Presence, that they become consumed with finding Him. Their longing for Him moves them to do what they would otherwise never do: Chase God. But what does it really mean to chase God? Can He be "caught"? Is there an end to the thirsting of man's soul for Him? Meet Tommy Tenney—God chaser. Join him in his search for God. Follow him as he ignores the maze of religious tradition and finds himself, not chasing God, but to his utter amazement, caught by the One he had chased.
ISBN 0-7684-2016-4

GOD CHASERS DAILY MEDITATION & PERSONAL JOURNAL
by Tommy Tenney.
ISBN 0-7684-2040-7

WOMEN ON THE FRONT LINES
by Michal Ann Goll.
History is filled with ordinary women who have changed the course of their generation. Here Michal Ann Goll, co-founder of Ministry to the Nations with her husband, Jim, shares how her own life was transformed and highlights nine women whose lives will impact yours! Every generation faces the same choices and issues; learn how you, too, can heed the call to courage and impact a generation.
ISBN 0-7684-2020-2

WORSHIP: THE PATTERN OF THINGS IN HEAVEN
by Joseph L. Garlington.
Worship and praise play a crucial role in the local church. Whether you are a pastor, worship leader, musician, or lay person, you'll find rich and anointed teaching from the Scriptures about worship! Joseph L. Garlington, Sr., a pastor, worship leader, and recording artist in his own right, shows how *worship is the pattern of things in Heaven*!
ISBN 1-56043-195-4

Other books you will enjoy reading

YOU HAVE NOT MANY FATHERS
by Dr. Mark Hanby with Craig Ervin.
Explore with Dr. Hanby the relationship of father and son as the foundational con-
nection for all spiritual impartation. As we turn our hearts toward one another, we
will recover our heritage of generational blessing and double-portion anointing!
ISBN 1-56043-166-0

YOU HAVE NOT MANY FATHERS STUDY GUIDE
by Dr. Mark Hanby with Craig Ervin.
ISBN 0-7684-2036-9

THE RENEWING OF THE HOLY GHOST
Do you need renewal? Everything in the natural, from birds to blood cells, must
either undergo a process of renewal or enter into death. Our spiritual life is no
different. With this book, your renewal can begin today!
ISBN 1-56043-031-1

If you would like to order any of these books or additional copies of *Hope for
Every Home* by John and Lee Guadagno, contact:

Sword of the Spirit Ministries
300 Kensington Avenue
Buffalo, New York 14214

Assoc. Pastor John A. Guadagno
hope4u@localnet.com